UNDERSTANDING GENDER IDENTITY

EXPLORE THE TRUE MEANING OF PRONOUNS AND GENDER DYSPHORIA, AND LEARN TO BE A MORE AUTHENTIC YOU

BRAXTON PHOENIX STOCK

To all the brave souls who have boldly challenged societal norms and expectations by exploring and embracing their gender identities. May this book serve as a beacon of hope and empowerment for those who are on their own journey of self-discovery, and may it inspire a world where every individual is free to express and celebrate their gender in all its beautiful diversity.

INTRODUCTION

It is revolutionary for any trans person to choose to be seen and visible in a world that tells us we should not exist.

Laverne Cox

I lived an unauthentic truth during the first 25 years of my life. Some of my first childhood memories clearly showed that I was not like other little girls. But not in the "not like other girls" trope sense, in a genuine and raw sense that made me feel confused and uncomfortable with my identity.

I didn't put on my mother's make-up in front of the mirror, trying to be just like her. I didn't want to be the princess, mermaid, or even the nanny holding the baby doll when my peers and I played pretend.

No, little me stood in front of the toilet trying to pee like Daddy. I would sneak into the bathroom and slather toothpaste across my tender little face, using the bristles of my toothbrush to "shave" the toothpaste off my cheeks like I'd seen my father do with his razor every other morning.

But still, despite the signs and behaviors that didn't fit my assigned gender, I lived on as the little girl everyone knew me to be—wearing my scruffy Mickey Mouse t-shirt and carrying a Pocahontas and John Smith Barbie doll.

As the years rolled on, something within me started to grow. It was an awareness that lingered in the back of my mind during every moment and interaction throughout my adolescent life. It was a nagging reminder that something was different about me. Something felt seriously wrong. I couldn't understand why the body I was born into felt so defective. My body was perfect and healthy. But it wasn't *me*.

Ignoring the blatant contrast within myself, puberty and the balancing act of being a teenage girl became a more prominent focal point for my disarray. I wasn't being honest with myself or those around me about how I felt. Pretending like I felt "normal" in any way became impossible to keep up with.

While I could have passed as a tomboy, always making friends with the "guys" and putting comfort before fashion, I knew my truth ran deeper. However, that didn't stop me from trying to fit in where I could.

Some years later, I was celebrating my 23rd birthday, still female, still pretending. The growing awareness in the back of my mind had become a burden too heavy to carry without setbacks. From the outside looking in, the average person would beg to differ, but I felt like I was operating someone else's empty vessel. And pretty soon, my outside reflected the burden too.

I stopped eating and turned to drugs for the only escape I could muster without taking my own life. It's not that I was necessarily suicidal, but I knew that facing the truth would send me down a path

I was terrified to face. It was unknown, and the risks seemed too high to throw away the only life I knew. So I chose to escape. I decided to run from the one thing that would - unbeknownst to me - make me feel whole. After all, what would "whole" even feel like? It wasn't something I'd ever truly felt before.

After a few years, slowly withering away any slither of authenticity I had, it all became too much. The healthy female body I once had became nothing but a near-death skeletal version. My mission to escape the painful reality I was living nearly led me to the end of it. I didn't want to die, but the weight of the now mountain-sized burden I carried was crushing me. Something had to give.

No longer willing to stay in denial, I decided to figure out what the hell was "wrong" with me. Then, after hours of research trying to explain my differences in any other way I could, I found something that helped me turn around and face the truth I was carrying. I stumbled across a trans masculine influencer on Instagram and felt confronted by the realization as it hit me.

I got up from the chair in my bedroom and walked to the dusty mirror I avoided every day. Looking into it felt like looking at myself in a dream—you know it's *you*, but something is off.

It was distressing to watch the final essence of the identity I'd tried to resonate with for so long become nothing but a smudge on the glass. It was painful, but as I began embracing who I truly am, I noticed something…

Like a game of smoke and mirrors, the colossal burden on my shoulders suddenly felt lighter, as if it had lifted away slightly. Perhaps the thing I thought was wrong with me was the one right thing I had denied myself for 25 years. The female persona I felt pressured to embody was a lie I had to embrace to fit the societal requirements associated with my sex.

My tears intensified as I released my tight grip on my female-presenting image. As liberating as this moment was, I had to face the all-consuming fear of what came next. But, even though I was scared, I decided this was it. From this moment onwards, I was ready to be my most authentic self. No matter how nervous I was to come out to my friends and family or what other judgments my journey would bring, I wouldn't look back.

It took some time, but after transitioning in a way that works best for me, I am proud to say I am transgender. With the help of the incredible people I have met at LGBTQ+ support groups and my sheer will and determination to change my life and live as my most authentic self, I am here, and I am happy.

Of course, this journey brings many ups and downs, some that I still have to face, no matter how comfortable I am in my own skin. But I want you to know that it's all WORTH IT. No amount of fear, judgment, or scrutiny should stop you from pursuing the life that you dream of. You, just like every other person on this planet, deserve to love and accept yourself.

Celebrities like Laverne Cox, whose powerful quote opened this book, Elliot Page, who faced society's judgment after the female characters they played won the hearts of millions, and Valentina Sampaio, who became the first openly trans model for Sports Illustrated and Victoria's Secret, have all been helping to pave the way forward.

Society is changing in a way that has opened the door for our true colors to fly out and make waves. We are creating - s p a c e - to just be. To be ourselves. To find each other. To find love and be happy in this world.

While it isn't perfect, the world is opening up. You don't have to sit alone in this experience anymore. Even if your story is nothing like mine or precisely like it, there is space for you. Whether you're questioning, 100% sure, or just curious, there is space for you. And if you're here to figure out where you stand on the spectrum of gender, there is space for you.

Life is not black and white. It seldom is. Life is full of spectrums and diversity; only society tries to categorize people and shove us into boxes. But we are part of society too, and it will never change if we don't set out to change it.

This book has eight chapters, each to uncover the various vital aspects of the transgender experience to help you figure out and embrace where you lie on the gender spectrum and what you can do to live a more authentic life.

The eight chapters include everything you need to know to get "up-to-speed" on gender, pronouns, dysphoria, and everything else in between. But most importantly, there are life-changing techniques and insights to help you navigate this bright new world with bravery, self-love, and understanding.

So please, I invite you to join me on this journey of self-exploration and discovery. Stay and uncover the authentic truth about gender identity to embrace where you stand within yourself. I promise you won't regret knowing yourself better, and I know that you'll look back after reading this book and feel the weight lifted off you too.

It won't always be easy, and you might face many bad days, but it will be worth it. I know because I've been where you are. However, I only wish to know that my journey and insights help bring peace to you. A peace that comes from understanding and loving yourself more. A peace that comes from living your most authentic life. And a sense of serenity comes from knowing you belong in this world.

So, let's get started and turn to chapter one, where we dive deep into the topic of gender, covering everything from gender roles, identities, and cultural influences on the gender binary, to how biological sex and gender genuinely relate.

I am so excited to be here with you and guide you through this incredibly transformative information. See you on the next page.

With love,

Braxton

AN IN-DEPTH EXPLORATION OF GENDER

I grew up in a small suburban town where gender was neither taught in school nor discussed at home. It was always a topic that was left vague and up to interpretation. Nevertheless, an underlying ideology has been drilled into us from birth: gender is binary.

From gender-reveal parties, where blue cakes mean a boy and pink cakes mean a girl, to boys being pushed to play with cars, while girls play dress-up and emulate household tasks for fun, these are just some ways Western culture has made the gender binary onto its society.

The early conditioning of children is the reason why little boys who want to wear dresses and girls who want to wear short hair for Halloween are ridiculed and labeled. No one who strays away from this binary brainwashing is safe from society's judgment. But it is time for that to change. Why? As a result of its deep roots in Western culture, the gender binary ideology is unsuited to inclusiveness.

Cultural Inclusion Of Gender Differences

Although natal sex is binary, where a male has XY chromosomes, and a female has XX, affecting their physical appearance and sexual organs, gender is a broad identification spectrum. You may identify at any point along this spectrum, from cisgender female to cisgender male, with the space in between representing your level of identification with either gender. It is also possible to identify outside of this spectrum entirely and be non-binary. Identifying as non-binary is where you do not associate or identify with either gender or find yourself having a more fluid relationship with gender.

In many ways, we have built our system on restricting people to labels rather than recognizing and providing labels for people to identify with and use comfortably. However, in some countries worldwide, the opposite is the case. Their gender system includes people's innate differences rather than trying to push the outlying people into one of two categories.

For example, Samoan culture has a recognized and accepted third gender, Fafa. People born biologically male but identify as female are known as Fa'afafine, and biological females who identify as male from a young age are known as Fa'afatamas. It is widely accepted as "normal" and celebrated in their culture. Many people with this third gender are not considered gay but embraced as the gender they identify with and lead everyday lives finding love and having families with people of the opposite gender identity.

Other cultures that adopt a similar recognition for transgender people include Thailand, which has a large population of a gender known as kathoey for people that Western civilization would consider transgender female, and Pakistan, India, Bangladesh, and Nepal, where transgender females are accepted and understood as a third gender known as hijras.

Understanding that gender is deeply rooted in culture while sex is rooted in biology gives us perspective on how Western culture has primarily shaped society to be less inclusive and generally reject gender differences. Culture tells people what to find acceptable or not. However, it is not always rooted in truth. The good news is that cultures can be shaped and more inclusive and accepting with time, information, and patience.

We've already experienced a massive shift towards inclusion, with surges of people stepping up, being brave, and telling their stories to spread awareness. Awareness brings understanding, and understanding brings acceptance. It is up to people living the transgender experience to speak up and make space in society for those who will come after them. That is why I am here writing this book. I want to help make space for you in our community and culture. I want you to feel like you can live authentically without worrying about anyone else's thoughts. Because the truth is, it doesn't matter what anyone else thinks.

Before transitioning, I felt the need to hide behind the image everyone knew and understood about me. I was scared to reveal the most authentic side of myself because I had been hiding it for so long. I was anxious people would assume this hidden side of myself was the fallacy while the version they all knew and loved was the reality. I had to learn that **people who genuinely love you won't need to understand it to accept it.** They already love the real you, no matter how hidden away you may feel.

And if you feel like you have no one, I promise there is a vast world of people out there who will welcome you with open arms. So don't worry about what the wrong people think when you're doing something that is right for you. Your authentic self will attract genuine friends and loved ones. Just focus on your journey and what resonates with you. Nothing else really matters. Not society's level of progression, not your one uncle's 2-cent opinion, and not the voice in your head that likes to break you down.

Trust your instincts and what you KNOW to be true about yourself; the rest will follow. If you're still figuring that out, don't worry, you've got time. By the end of this book, I know you will have taken steps toward loving and accepting yourself so that the world can follow suit. But before you can move forward and see where you stand, you must understand that gender is fluid. There is a difference between your gender identity and your gender expression.

Gender Identity Vs. Gender Expression

Gender identity is how you identify with yourself on the inside; it's how you feel your gender to be. It pertains to which gender you identify as and if you identify with a gender at all.

For example, if you are a cisgender female, you will be assigned a female at birth based on your sex, and you will resonate with your assigned gender. If you are a transgender woman, you will have been assigned male at birth, but you deeply feel and have a knowing inside yourself that you are female. And if you are non-binary, you may feel no resonance with either gender or feel differently gendered at different times in your life. You might prefer the label non-binary to avoid having either gender's stereotypes assigned to you by society.

Gender expression is how you express your identity to the world. It's how you appear to others. You might feel a significant disconnect if you are transgender and have not transitioned or come out to family and friends about your gender identity.

A great example of gender expression and how it relates to gender identity is when cis-gendered males wear dresses, as Harry Styles did on the cover of the December 2020 issue of Vogue, or when cis-gendered females have buzz cuts, like Natalie Portman in 2006 for her role in V for Vendetta. Although they expressed themselves in stereotypical ways of the opposite sex, it does not govern their gender identity.

How you express yourself outside does not affect or change your gender identity. However, it can help you to convey to those around you which gender you identify as using society's stereotypical images of male or female. The most general example is when a transgender woman grows out long hair and starts wearing make-up to present more feminine in society and feel more connected to her gender identity.

You can see how gender expression doesn't end with the transgender community. Everyone expresses gender in some way, but not always how society expects. Society can get a bit tricky here when it comes to expressing yourself and how you want to be treated by others.

For example, a cisgender female who has short hair and dresses more androgynous might be confused by the public as being male or trans-gender. The truth is they are neither and identify as female. In the same way, a transgender male might still have some feminine quali-ties in their appearance and be mistaken for a woman by the public. Non-binary people can also appear more masculine or feminine on the outside but not identify with either gender or identify with both genders.

Even though it can be frustrating and sometimes offensive to see the public make mistakes, it is essential to be the change we want to see, which means having patience with people and kindly explaining the truth or correcting people constructively.

Before I transitioned, I predominantly expressed myself by presenting as more masculine. Since I can remember, I've worn men's clothing and abstaining from make-up. I even made damn sure my nails were cut super short, as any length to my fingernails made me think: woman. Girly was so far off from what I, someone who had not embraced my authentic truth of being a transmasculine man, wanted to show the world. In many ways, my gender expres-sion was one of the only chances to show how I identified with myself and express that to society. However, even after starting my transition, I was still mistaken for a female until I acquired more traditionally masculine traits like facial hair.

Even though it was disheartening at times, I quickly realized I couldn't blame people for making assumptions they learned in childhood or for learning too slowly. Everyone has their focus in life, and most people rely on society to tell them what they should accept and what is "weird" or worth scrutiny.

Even though I was not wearing pink-flowy dresses, my face was softer, and most people had known me as female for most of my life. I realized that it was up to me to stay as steady and stable within myself and my identity as possible so as not to let the comments and mistakes of others govern how I feel or how I see myself. I knew that over time, people would have to get past it and would learn how to address me correctly.

Society is also changing rapidly, so I figured that getting myself worked up and hurt by someone's uneducated comment wasn't worth it. Of course, being misgendered can trigger dysphoria, but this is something I had to work through and accept as part of my journey instead of blaming others for their mistakes.

So remember, just because you present more masculine, and enjoy doing so, doesn't necessarily mean you are transgender. Conversely, you can present as more feminine and be a transgender man. There are no set rules for how you should or shouldn't express your gender other than doing what makes you happy. How you identify within yourself is what matters most. Getting to the bottom of this truth is how you can embrace every fiber of YOU and express yourself accordingly.

Once you have confidence in yourself and your identity, it won't matter what others say or think. And if someone judges you from a binary, stereotypical perspective, try to see that they have either made a mistake based on their worldview or are uneducated about the transgender experience. It can take some time, but keep it in your mind as you embark on this journey of self-discovery.

The Fluidity of Gender Roles

This book will revisit how you can grow your inner stability and express your authentic self without fear. As we go and continue discussing these essential topics, the goal is for your mind to become rich with knowledge as your emotions and thoughts untie into a validated and harmonious state.

The more you know and the more you understand about yourself, the more in line you are going to feel within your gender identity, your gender expression, and what gender role you feel the need to embody.

Gender roles are traditionally based on the expected social presentation of people in a binary framework. They are based on the stereotypes of feminine women and masculine men and leave no room for non-confirming people, both cis and transgender. A woman, for instance, is expected to care for her children and be a homemaker. Conversely, men are expected to be leaders, warriors, and breadwinners, with no room for men and women to pursue or present otherwise comfortably.

In the modern era within Western culture, you can already see a significant shift in stereotypical gender roles compared to before the 1900s. More women pursue careers in predominantly male-run industries, and more men are stay-at-home fathers than ever before. According to an article in Forbes magazine titled "The Rise Of The Stay-At-Home Dad," numbers for stay-at-home dads have risen by 8% since 1989. The report also states that this rise predominantly stems from women out-earning their husbands.

While society slowly expands to allow for more fluidity between gender roles, as the feminist movement strongly continues, the LGBTQ+ community has had the space to form and emerge as part of a healthier society—a society now more inclusive to people who naturally do not fit the stereotypical gender roles. Of course, we still have a way to go, but we're progressing.

Even though the feminist movement was officially recognized to start in 1848 at the Seneca Falls Convention, many men and women have been standing up for equality between genders since ancient times. A great example of this is the story of Mulan. Yes, I know the Disney variation was only released in 1998, but the original story of Mulan is based on a true story from the Northern Wei Dynasty of China between 386 CE-536 CE.

The story of Mulan is inspiring for our society as it pushes against the gender binary and proves a powerful point with a patriarchy-busting heroine that stands up for change and inclusivity.

In a nutshell, Mulan is a straight, cis woman suppressed by her family and forced into the stereotypical view of society, where women are only regarded as valuable when they are subservient, kind, and physically attractive to win a husband. However, when she sees her elderly father's name on the call list for war, she secretly takes his place dressed up as a male soldier.

Mulan ultimately saves the whole of China after training with the other soldiers and proving everyone wrong. She demonstrates that a woman can do what a man can do and even be the story's heroine due to her sheer determination and love for her father. She shows that when women are given equal rights, they can have a more significant, more profound impact on the progression of society and that there is more value to a woman than mere looks and subservience.

She gains the respect of many soldiers while disguised as one of them. Still, even when they reveal her true identity, she remains an inspiration to the friends she's made, some of whom dress up as concubines in a palace raid scene during the Disney adaptation.

With the example of Mulan, you can see how gender roles can damage society as they put limitations on both men and women. Of course, there are some truths to gender roles based on masculinity and femininity's qualities, behaviors, and tendencies. Still, they should not govern our expectations of people based on gender.

The Biology Behind Gender

You now know sex has little to do with gender, and gender does not govern anyone's gender expression or behavior. Nor does it set the stage for gender roles to control behavior, occupations, or appearances.

The same goes for female and male brains; they each show general differences that support some gender roles and stereotypes. However, this should not be taken as black and white but as generalizations for masculine and feminine qualities in male and female brains. Again, brains can exhibit many differences that can affect this presentation.

For example, generally, female brains have a bigger prefrontal cortex, orbital frontal cortex, superior temporal cortex, lateral parietal cortex, and insula, while male brains have larger ventral temporal and occipital regions. The difference is significant enough that a classifier can identify male and female brains using MRI imagery at an accuracy rate above 85%.

According to a recent study in the Journal of Clinical Medicine, "Brain Sex in Transgender Women Is Shifted towards Gender Identity," (2022) using MRI scans to compare and identify cisgender and transgender brains, transgender brains are more likely to appear closer to the gender the person identifies as.

The study compared the brain scans of 24 cisgender men, 24 cisgender women, and 24 transgender women. The scans were sorted by a classifier that identified brain sex, with "male" and "female" placed on a spectrum of zero to one. Note: the trans women in the study had never taken hormone replacement therapy, so the results were based on natural brain formation.

While the computer was largely accurate with the cisgender brain images, something groundbreaking happened with the transgender brain scans. When the computer attempted to identify the sex of the trans women's brains, although they were still mostly appearing male, they were significantly closer to that of a cis female than in comparison to the cis male's brain scans.

These results suggest something significant to validating the trans experience: Being transgender is something you are born with, not influenced only by social or environmental input.

Although cisgender brains are also varying between the two typical presentations of "male" and "female," the sway towards "female" in transwoman is undeniable. From a biological perspective, this can explain why trans people experience a feeling or know that they are a different gender from what they were assigned at birth. It shows us that the external presentation of sex does not always coincide with gender identity and that your chosen gender identity is largely biological and not necessarily a choice.

It is also essential to understand and accept that there are reasons why females, in general, take more naturally to specific occupations, styles of dressing, and behavioral traits. In contrast, males take more naturally to others. However, this shouldn't close the door or set limitations for biological sex, gender, or gender expression. Either sex or gender can exhibit any level of both masculine or feminine traits.

We'll get into the topic of gender stereotypes in more depth in chapter four, but for now, try to release the expectations you may feel and move on with an open mind.

What feels right to you is not a choice; it is your authentic experience of the world and how you associate with it. It's important to note, however, that you *do* have choices. You have the choice to express your true nature and live more authentically. These choices include but are not limited to changing your name to something you resonate with more deeply, opening up to the world if you want to, and coming out to family when you choose to. Your power lies in your ability to express yourself fully. So, live it, love it, and take what people say with a pinch of salt.

The Art of Dressing in Drag

A great example of how people can thrive while expressing themselves outside of gender norms is the art of drag. Drag is an art open to anyone. While it is practiced mainly by cis men and trans women, some cis women and trans men also enjoy drag. It is a form of performance art where traditionally gay men dress up as women, mainly in a bright, exaggerated way.

People who do drag, usually known as drag queens, often have unique personas and character. When performed by cis women or trans men dressing as an exaggerated male persona, these characters are called drag kings. Performers choose fun names with a play on words and use them to have fun and be someone else for a night. Most drag queens or kings are unrecognizable from their everyday selves, which is all part of the practice.

It's also worth noting that dressing in drag and being transgender are entirely different. Drag is a style of performance art while being transgender and changing one's appearance to fit the gender norms of society, or otherwise, is gender identity and expression.

Drag might be a newer term, but the practice of men dressing up and performing as female characters is nothing modern. The tradition originates from Shakespearean times when women were forbidden to perform, so men had to play female roles. This was not considered drag back then, and the reasoning behind the practice is entirely different. However, it just shows how there's nothing outlandish about people dressing up and performing as the opposite gender.

The exclusion of women is not what drag stands for today. Instead, it is an art form that fights society's gender norms. Drag was popularized in the modern era, but the first drag queen was Princess Seraphina in the 18th century, acting as a messenger for gay men, a "crime" that men could be hanged for back then.

Before drag became drag, it was known as the art of vaudeville, a comical theater style, frequently including pantomime, dialogue, dancing, and singing. But in the early 20th century, when drag queens started gaining more individual popularity, the art broke away from vaudeville and became its own thing. It was cleverly named after the dresses the queens would wear as they dragged on the floor behind them.

Time and time again, people that would now be seen as part of the LGBTQ+ community have been sticking up for gender differences or breaking gender stereotypes for centuries. Non-binary people also practice the art.

Exploring Non-Binary Identity

Before we go any further, I want to clarify something about being non-binary. Even though the term is relatively new, it is merely an inclusive modern label for gender non-conforming.

While I have mostly referred to myself and identified as a trans man, the more I unfold my gender identity and expression, the more I realize I feel more resonant with being a non-binary, transmasculine person. This is because there are so many days where I don't feel like any gender at all, regardless of how masculine I present myself to the world. I see myself and *feel* like I'm simply a human that doesn't fit into either box.

Many trans people feel sure about their gender identity and feel a sense of solidity in it. On the other hand, non-binary people tend to feel more fluidity within their gender identity or not resonate with either gender at all.

Knowing where you fit is sometimes a bit complicated, but just know that it is a personal part of your identity to uncover and doesn't change your belonging or value within the LGBTQ+ community or the rest of the world. If you aren't sure and have spent your life up until this point outwardly identifying as cisgender, transgender, or non-binary but have since discovered a more authentic truth about how you identify, don't let that stop you from adjusting and expressing yourself how you truly need to.

Although society has a history of prejudice and judgment against anyone non-conforming, in the larger sense of the word, try to see the places in society where differences are being openly expressed and celebrated.

For example, Elliot Page spent most of their life as a well-known, presumably cisgender actress. Before transitioning, some of their most iconic roles included Whip It, Inception, and Juno, where he played a young teenage girl who accidentally fell pregnant and went through with the birth.

With a reputation like Elliot's, I can only imagine how brave he had to be to come out as transgender to his family, friends, and fans in

December 2020. He has stated that his pronouns are he/they and has since transitioned.

Not only is he leading a great example of health and happiness for the trans community, but he has also received tremendous celebrity support, showing just how far our society is progressing.

The Trans Gender Identities

Transgender is an umbrella term for a list of gender identities. Knowing and understanding the list of inclusive labels will help you better identify your gender and find others who can relate more wholeheartedly. Each person across the trans community is so unique from the next that one label will not fully serve everyone. However, the term transgender is there to contain the different gender identities.

To recap, the two base gender categories are cisgender and transgender. Since we know what both of those mean, we can now get into the sub-labels for genders that fall under the transgender umbrella.

Binary

- **Transman:** A person born female that identifies as male.
- **Transwoman:** A person born male that identifies as female.

Non-binary

- **Gender fluid:** A person whose gender moves outside or between the binary gender expectations.

- **Gender expansive:** A person whose gender goes beyond their cultural standard of gender, who wants to broaden the cultural expectations of their gender.
- **Demigender:** A person who only identifies partially with a specific gender identity. Example: Demigirl, demiboy, demi-androgyne.
- **Genderqueer:** A person whose gender identity doesn't align with societal expectations of gender. It is also used by people who identify with multiple gender identities.
- **Gender outlaw:** A person who refuses to let society define their gender.
- **Androgyne:** A person who identifies as both male and female simultaneously.
- **Agender:** A person who does not identify with either male or female, and sometimes no gender at all.
- **Bigender:** A person who identifies with two genders.
- **Omnigender:** A person who identifies with and experiences all genders.
- **Pangender/polygender:** A person who identifies with and experiences parts of some genders or more than one gender.

Gender is a spectrum with enough room to include every gender identity someone can feel. There is no set rule for identifying based on your biology, and there are no limitations to how you should express yourself in that identity.

Again, within the trans and cisgender communities, gender expression can vary widely and may have little to do with someone's gender identity. You can very well be a non-binary, bigender person who chooses to express themselves more femininely without needing to identify as a woman. You can be a cis male who loves to dress in drag and perform every weekend without the need to identify as trans or gay.

If you are like many other gender non-conforming people and me, and you haven't fully discovered or pinpointed exactly what labels or gender expression work for you, please know there is no pressure or hurry to do so. Instead, treat this process like a journey of self-discovery and get excited to know yourself better.

This journey, although sometimes challenging and admittedly confusing, doesn't have to be serious all the time. You can enjoy this process and indulge in every positive change or experience that it brings.

Now that we've emerged after that deep dive into gender identity and expression, meet me on the next page in chapter two. We will go even deeper into sex and sexuality, answering the pressing question of "Are they the same thing?"

We already know that biological sex has nothing to do with gender identity or expression, so now let me explain why and how sex and sexual orientation differ as well.

2

DEFINING SEX AND SEXUALITY: UNDERSTANDING THE KEY DIFFERENCES

There is a possibility that you might feel uncomfortable reading this chapter. I say this because it's not easy for me to talk about something so personal that I rarely discuss in my everyday life—my sex and sexuality.

Sex, in any sense of the word, has been a taboo subject for generations. Whether it refers to intercourse, genitals, or sexual orientation, it is a private, personal subject that is usually better kept between romantic partners and doctors. However, I will be very real with you here for self-discovery and vulnerability.

This book is here to explore the nitty-gritty, make you feel something real, and show you that whatever you've got going on inside yourself, outside yourself, and about yourself, you can accept and love yourself as a whole.

I'm still learning to do this, but I wouldn't be where I am today without taking the plunge and embracing my sex, gender, gender expression, and sexuality. In this process, it helps to recognize that while these four topics are firmly linked, they do not define each other.

Like four links to the same chain, sex, gender, gender expression, and sexuality are interconnected and can influence each other in many ways. But this influence needs to be more rigid to stop fluidity. Even a solid metal chain still has give-and-take; there is still room for movement, flow, and variation.

Although I was assigned female at birth and lived most of my youth this way, my sex and sexuality seemed to create a back-and-forth within me. While mainly expressing myself in a very masculine sense, I was still seen as and considered a girl by those around me and myself.

I didn't understand that even though I deeply didn't feel like a girl, express myself as a girl, or see myself as a girl, I could be anything different. So all seemed completely fine and acceptable when I was attracted to the boys around me, especially living in a town where being gay or different was not quite acceptable.

For a while, looking back, I justified this attraction as potential envy for their gender. After all, for the most part, they were everything I identified with. I dressed like them, enjoyed spending time with them more than the other girls, and I resonated with their gender so much more than my own. However, after some reflection, it is easy to see that I only felt attracted to certain boys for who they were, not because they were male. Their gender never occurred to me then, and I was too young to know anything about sex.

Nonetheless, although I felt different in my sexuality, everyone around me saw a young girl crushing on the boys in her class. No one questioned anything, not even me, not until my attraction transformed as I got older to include girls as well. After that, things started to get more confusing for me, and the labels of my sexuality began to matter.

As someone who didn't know they were trans, being a female attracted to other girls naturally earned me the label of "lesbian."

Not only was being lesbian extremely frowned upon where I'm from, but it didn't feel right. I realized I didn't see myself as a girl attracted to other girls. Rather, I felt like a young man attracted to the feminine qualities of women. But at this point, I wasn't, so why did I feel like that?

I can't stress enough how coming across a book like this would've helped me at that point in my life. I had no understanding of what being transgender was. The way I was raised made how I felt seem impossible. It felt so wrong, even though it came naturally to me. I didn't understand how something I had no control over could dub me an outcast within seconds of sharing how I felt. But I knew it would, so I kept quiet until it was almost too late.

Burying an integral part of who you are will make you sick. It made me sick, and I didn't think I could ever be happy. But being gentle with yourself and figuring out how you identify will improve everything. Sure, maybe at first you will have to go through a rocky patch, like coming out to friends and family or going through a transition, but you weren't born to please others.

You were born the way you are to take up space and express yourself. You were born to love and be loved. So read closely here, and understand that the way you truly and naturally identify is authentic for you. That is how you were meant to be before society or culture told you you couldn't. Being transgender is real; above all, it is not a defect, disorder, or violation. Being transgender is NATURAL.

Now that I have understood that and can love myself for it, I feel free to explore and learn about my sexuality. I feel free enough to be me and share my differences with you so you can do the same. There is no one else that you can be better than perfectly you.

The Spectrum Of Sexuality

I know that sexuality is often more complex than simply being gay or straight. Just like gender identity and expression, sexuality is on a spectrum too! Remember the chain analogy? Likewise, sex can be viewed on a spectrum, like gender and sexuality. The three are more similar than you might think.

Think about how different any physical attribute of humans can be, how different everyone's height, muscle mass, eye color, or hair formation is. The truth about biological sex is that it includes male, female, AND intersex people.

Being intersex, better known as people with a difference of sexual development (DSD), is when someone has a combination of male and female sex characteristics. Sex characteristics don't end and begin with genitalia, either. After puberty, they include secondary sex characteristics such as widened hips in women and facial hair in men. There is no limit to how far someone's sex characteristics can sway to the opposite sex, which is why I say that sex is also on a spectrum.

Other factors that influence sex include hormones, genetics, and chromosomes. These, too, can differ widely between the sex classifications, with males sometimes having traces of or a significant amount of female characteristics, females having some or a lot of male features, or people having a relatively balanced mix of both.

Biological sex is defined and assigned at birth based on someone's overall sexual genotype and phenotype. According to the Neuroscience 2nd Edition book, sexual genotype refers to the person's XX or XY sex-determining chromosomes, and sexual phenotype refers to the person's internal and external genitalia, secondary sex characteristics, and behavior.

The book states: "If everything proceeds according to plan during development, the XX genotype leads to a person with ovaries, oviducts, uterus, cervix, clitoris, labia, and vagina—i.e., a phenotypic female. Similarly, the XY genotype leads to a person with testicles, epididymis, vas deferens, seminal vesicles, penis, and scrotum—i.e., a phenotypic male."

However, the book also explains that 1-2% of all babies are born with intersex traits. While the variations in a person with a DSD's phenotype can vary slightly to significantly, it can also include genotypic variations such as someone with XO, XXY, or XYY chromosomes.

While some intersex people have different sex-determining chromosomes, many people with a DSD have typical XX or XY chromosome combinations, only showing variation in their physical sex characteristics. These include hormone differences, variations in genitals, and behavioral traits.

Having a DSD can also influence brain development and structure, causing people who appear predominantly female on the outside to have a brain structure associated with more masculine traits. It can cause people to feel and behave more like the "opposite sex."

I am mentioning all of this because although this circumstance sounds similar to the trans experience, they are entirely different. Yes, someone with a DSD can most definitely identify as transgender or cisgender, but I want to show you just how diverse our biology is. It's easy to accept that our identity can be on a spectrum, but we are often not taught how biology can be non-binary too. Let me repeat that: Our biology is non-binary too.

The LGBTQ+ community is inclusive to everyone, including people with a DSD. Some community variations include "I" for intersex in the label—i.e., LGBTQIA+. There are, of course, similarities between the general transgender experience and the experience of those with intersex traits, such as gender dysphoria. However, the key difference is that intersex refers to variations in sex characteristics, while transgender relates to gender identity variations.

So if you already know that sex refers to the physical attributes that help doctors assign you as male, female, or intersex at birth, and gender refers to how you identify within yourself and the world, how does sexuality fit into this dynamic?

The Sexuality Link

I was confused for the longest time about how I indeed identified. First, it was, "I'm a girl attracted to boys. That's pretty normal, isn't it?" Then it became, "Oh no, I'm attracted to girls too, but I *can't* be a lesbian because I'm not *really* a girl, am I?" Without the knowledge I have now, understanding how I identified and how I could describe it seemed hopeless.

For years I questioned my sexuality, feeling like the only boxes I could fit into were: Straight, Gay, Lesbian, or Bisexual. The only trouble was I didn't resonate with ANY of the "appropriate" labels. I wasn't a cis girl attracted to other girls, I wasn't a cis boy attracted to other boys, and I definitely didn't feel like a cis girl attracted to boys. When I discovered that I am trans, my whole world *transformed* into the life that I live and love today.

As I unfolded the knowledge found within the LGBTQ+ community, both online and in person, I quickly learned that there is more to sexuality than four basic boxes. There are currently at least 20 different sexualities, each with criteria to help you better understand and label yours.

Sexuality is how you experience sexual and romantic attraction. In contrast, sex refers to your biological identity, gender refers to your gender identity, and gender expression refers to how you express your gender identity. There is no rule as to how your sexuality should fit with any of the other links to the identity chain.

For example, suppose you are a transgender woman, who expresses herself in a more masculine way. In that case, you can still identify as heterosexual, meaning you are sexually and romantically attracted to men, despite expressing yourself in a more masculine way.

Growing up expressing myself in a very masculine way, knowing deep down that I wasn't cis or straight, gave me a bit of a bias at first. I felt like it made sense that I was gender diverse if you were looking at me from the outside. So I very much expressed my masculine gender—it was almost obvious.

However, because of my experience with gender expression, I felt confused about how my aunt, Margie, identified. Seeing her hoop earrings dangle beneath her buzzcut hair, wearing woman's slacks and an androgynous shirt made me question whether she was like me. From the outside, Aunt Margie gave the appearance of society's stereotypical lesbian, but she was, and still is, a happy cis woman married to my uncle.

The similarities between my aunt and I are a great example of how you can't tell someone's sexuality just by looking at them. It's also a great example of how you can express your gender identity in any way you want without worrying about what's "right" or "wrong" for your gender identity.

The most well-known sexual orientations recognized in society are heterosexuality, bisexuality, gay/lesbian, and asexuality. While these labels can cover a broader spectrum of sexual identities, you can deviate from these to any degree. However, unlike other spectrums, like sex, where you have opposites on each side, sexuality's spectrum is a little different. The spectrum of sexuality looks more like a color wheel, with every variation bleeding into the next.

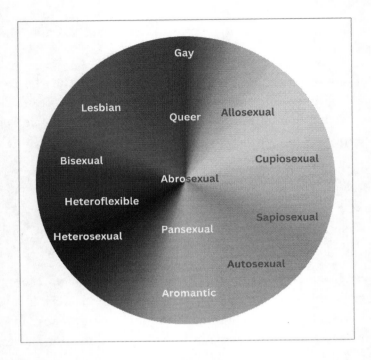

Another thing to note about sexuality is that it is fluid. Your sexuality can change over time, which is absolutely normal and can happen to anyone regardless of environmental factors or experiences. This is probably a good time to mention that, just like sex and gender identity, sexuality is **not a choice**.

Even though some people believe that being anything but heterosexual *is* a choice, your sexuality is a natural occurrence based on various factors out of your control. While it is often defined in relation to your own sex or gender identity, most scientists agree that sexual orientation is a combined result of biological, environmental, hormonal, and emotional factors.

However, no matter what your sexual identity is, you do have a choice regarding it—embracing and *accepting* your sexuality for what it is and not for what society or family says it should be. That choice includes letting go of the pressure to fit in and not seeing cisgender, heterosexual people as "normal" or anyone who deviates from that as "different."

Any variation of sexual and gender identity, gender expression, or sex IS normal because it naturally occurs in people from all walks of life. I won't explain how or why we have been led to believe otherwise. However, I will say this: Although it can be a lonely journey at times, and although there is still much hate and close-mindedness in the world, now is the perfect time in history to bring the truth about gender identity, sexuality, sex, and gender expression to light. With the help of social media and the internet, we can express ourselves, share our authentic experiences with others, and come together to form accessible, inclusive communities within society.

It is proven that people in the LGBTQ+ community have a higher risk for mental health problems and suicide. Given that this increased risk is often due to a lack of belonging and unaccepting family members, it shows just how important it is to change society worldwide.

Sexuality starts developing and presenting itself during teenagehood, meaning that teenagers and young adults who do not fit the current norms are often mistreated and misunderstood. After growing up with a sense of "wrongness" and often having family disown them, it is no surprise that people in our community feel like they don't belong.

This is why I am so passionate about changing the narrative for people in the LGBTQ+ community. We would not need separation or classification in a perfect world just to feel included. But I am proud to add this book to the growing number of available resources, helping improve society. I hope that one day there will be no need for communities to separate from the general society and that we can all love and accept each other no matter how much we differ.

I'm speaking from experience here, as I was one of those people carrying around a sense of wrongness about who I really am. For the longest time, I hid it away from everyone around me, including myself. One of the last things I had to accept about myself after coming out as trans and embracing my transition was my sexuality.

When you grow up in a conservative area, as I did, any identity that strays away from heterosexual cisgender is frowned upon. I know that if being different from this gender and sexuality "norm" were more accepted and understood where I come from, I would not have been so quick to hate myself, hideaway, and turn to drugs as an escape. I am sad that it had to take me getting to such a low point before I could love and accept myself, but hopefully, my journey can help you get there a lot quicker.

After much thought and self-understanding, I can comfortably explore my sexuality. I have so far found interest in the label of abro-sexuality, but I am still figuring my sexuality out. I want you to know that it's okay to do that, by the way. You can flow with your sexuality and allow it to unfold before you like a lotus emerging from murky waters.

You don't have to have everything about yourself figured out to be valid in your experience. Feel free to use labels that feel comfortable for you, and if you find better labels that you resonate with more at a later stage, don't be afraid to change them. Remember, sexuality is fluid! With that said, let's get into the various known sexual identities.

The A-Z of Sexual Orientation

- **Abrosexual:** A person who has the ability to have varying or fluid levels of sexual or romantic attraction throughout one's life as well as changes in sexual orientation.

- **Allosexual:** A person who experiences sexual attraction.
- **Androsexual:** A person sexually or romantically attracted to men, males, or masculinity.
- **Aromantic:** A person who experiences little to no romantic attraction, regardless of gender.
- **Autosexual:** A person who is sexually attracted to themselves.
- **Autoromantic:** A person who finds their relationship with themselves to be romantic or is romantically attracted to themselves.
- **Bicurious:** A person curious to explore bisexual experiences.
- **Bisexual:** A person who is sexually, romantically, or emotionally attracted to more than one gender.
- **Biromantic:** A person who experiences only romantic attraction to more than one gender.
- **Cupiosexual:** An asexual person who doesn't experience sexual attraction but still wants to engage in sexual activity.
- **Demiromantic:** A person who can only experience romantic attraction after specific circumstances, such as forming a strong emotional or sexual connection with someone.
- **Demisexual:** A person who does not experience a sexual attraction towards anyone unless under a specific set of circumstances, such as forming a strong emotional or romantic connection with someone first.
- **Gay:** A person having an emotional, romantic, or sexual attraction to people who share the same gender identity as you. It can be used by men and women, both cis and trans, or non-binary people.
- **Gynesexual:** A person sexually or romantically attracted to women, females, or femininity.

- **Heteroflexible:** A person who considers themselves to be heterosexual but may experience a situational attraction that deviates from that.
- **Heterosexual:** A person who is sexually, romantically, or emotionally attracted to people of the "opposite" gender identity, i.e., Females to males, males to females, including both cis and transgender identities.
- **Lesbian:** A woman or non-binary person attracted to women. However, some lesbian people prefer to use "Gay" instead.
- **Pansexual:** A person with the potential for sexual, emotional, or romantic attraction towards people of any gender or sexual identity.
- **Panromantic:** A person with the potential for romantic or emotional attraction towards people of any gender or sexual identity.
- **Queer:** An umbrella sexuality referring to people who are not exclusively heterosexual. The term is used by people who believe sexuality to be on a spectrum and not necessarily divided into solid sexuality categories.
- **Questioning:** A person exploring their sexual identity.
- **Sapphic:** A woman or a female-identifying person who is attracted to other women or female-identifying people. The term is commonly used to describe lesbians, bisexuals, non-binary individuals, cis women, mascs, and trans femmes.
- **Sapiosexual:** A person attracted to others based on their intelligence, not gender.
- **Skoliosexual:** A person sexually, emotionally, or romantically attracted to non-binary people.
- **Spectrasexual:** A person sexually or romantically attracted to multiple or varied gender identities, but not necessarily all or any of them.

This list of sexualities is current in this book, but please note that it is ever-expanding and shifting. If you did not resonate with any of the above labels, go with your gut and keep exploring! You don't have to feel like your experience isn't valid just because it may not fit any description or box. We're all human, and these labels are only here to help us better identify and express ourselves.

If you did find a label that fits you and feel excited or validated, I urge you to share it with somebody you can trust. It might feel scary, but I want you to feel like your sexuality is something you can express openly, even if it is only to your best friend at first. You can even feel free to E-mail me at brax.phoenix.stock@gmail.com if you feel you have no one you can turn to.

One of my favorite actresses growing up, Raven-Simoné, is a celebrity who feared sharing her sexuality with the world. After being a Disney actor for many years and starring in other famous TV shows like The Cosby Show, she didn't want to feel judged by her huge following. However, after some encouragement from a co-star, and much contemplation, she realized that by sharing that she is gay, she could help expand the societal view on queer identities and help build a more inclusive world.

It is important to be open about yourself for others to understand and love you authentically. Even if the wrong people don't want to hear you or understand you, the right people will listen. Better yet, someone struggling may be listening and feel represented by something you say or do.

For example, if you are trans or queer and create incredible art, being open about your journey can help others feel included and can show others that there is space for them.

Get comfortable using your voice to be proud of who you are and what you stand for. That is the only way our society will move forward and become the inclusive place we want it to be. We don't have to get upset or make a lot of noise to get our point across, but we do have to be patient and consistent, like a river slowly shaping a rock.

One of the ways our community can thrive in society is by learning the correct way to use pronouns. If we can get it right, it also makes it that much easier for other people. So turn to chapter three to learn the importance of pronouns and how to use them correctly.

3
PRONOUNS: HOW OUR LANGUAGE SHAPES GENDER IDENTITY

Tapping my pencil against the desk to the rhythm of the Green Day song I had in my mind on repeat, I stared out the classroom window. Then, with a huff of frustration, my English teacher, Mrs. Rini, yelled my name.

Hearing my name gave me a funny feeling. I knew it was mine, but it felt borrowed. I winced at the sound of it and quickly brought my attention to the chalkboard.

"The girl ate her apple then threw the core away herself."

On the board was a lesson about pronouns in the English language and how "he/him" belongs to boys and "she/her" belongs to girls. There was nothing else to it. Although I was only a child in primary school, the lesson made me feel uncomfortable for reasons I didn't understand.

Now that the world is changing and inclusion is becoming a pressing issue for society, I feel uncomfortable because the lesson continued to instill the idea that gender is binary, and that's final. The lesson instilled an ideology that didn't leave room for how I identified.

Even though I was still living as a young girl with no concept of what being transgender meant, I knew what the pronouns "she/her" implied about me, and I didn't feel comfortable with that. Hearing my name had a similar effect on me.

Since I've started my transition and changed my name to one that fits my identity better, I understand why pronouns are necessary to get right in our society. Just like a name, pronouns help us identify ourselves and others correctly.

It wasn't Mrs. Rini's fault that her lesson made a young student feel like they didn't belong. Instead, the responsibility lies in the system of society—a society that continues to push a binary ideal on gender relentlessly.

While things are different now, society and its language were not designed for inclusivity in the years I was in school. And when you don't leave room for people and their differences, you open up opportunities for prejudice and outcast.

That is why it's so important for us to make an effort to transition society and the language we use to become more authentic to how people naturally are. Nature is not binary. There is always flow and spectrum to it. You can't force nature into a rigid box of ideals where you can only see things in black or white. The world is colorful, so we must expand our terminology, language, and thinking to include every shade.

The Problem With Gendered Language

Just like my teacher so casually taught the school curriculum with no reason to consider whether it was inclusive, we continue to use gendered language without even thinking about it. It is so ingrained in us that it's automatic.

The problem with gendered language is that it is still set up to push the gender binary. We have been taught to rely on someone's perceived gender identity to decide which pronouns to use for them without question. As a result, we unconsciously refer to someone as he/him if the person appears male and she/her if the person appears female.

Gendered language can also perpetuate harmful gender stereotypes, such as assumptions about what roles and behaviors are appropriate for men and women. For example, phrases like "man up" or "act like a lady" reinforce harmful stereotypes about how men and women should behave and can contribute to toxic masculinity and sexism.

For example, if you order coffee at a restaurant and your server wears makeup, you might sit at your table and say, "She was so friendly when I tipped her for the coffee." You might not have given it a second thought, but you automatically gendered your server and assumed their pronouns.

So what, where's the harm in that, right? If your server identifies as male, using he/him pronouns, he might go home and feel misunderstood. He might become dysphoric about his gender identity and feel depressed from being misgendered by all his customers because our society is not set up for inclusion, variation from the binary, or freedom of self-expression.

What if your name is James, but everyone keeps calling you Jake? You know your name is James, and you identify with James. However, everyone keeps calling you Jake. You might feel upset, confused, and gaslighted about your name.

Using gender-neutral language can be a way to be more inclusive and respectful of all individuals, regardless of their gender identity. Gender-neutral language refers to words and phrases that do not imply a specific gender, such as "they" or "them" instead of "he" or "she" or "partner" instead of "husband" or "wife."

So, with these examples in mind, isn't it strange how everyone can accept a name in seconds and have no problem if someone corrects them for getting it wrong, but pronouns can still be an issue for so many people to accept?

The truth is, someone's pronouns should be just as essential to get correct as their name. There are thousands of names worldwide, and you can remember hundreds of them, including whose name belongs to whom. So why should it be more challenging to remember a small handful of pronouns and who uses which ones?

Just like it isn't up to us to decide what name to call someone, it isn't up to us to gender someone and decide which pronouns we would like to use for them. Even if you don't think someone's pronouns suit how you view them, you should always use someone's proper pronouns out of respect and inclusion.

If you don't think someone's name suits them, you would unlikely say that out loud or refuse to call them by it; you would simply accept their name and use it regardless. Pronouns are no different.

How to Use Pronouns

The use of pronouns is crucial within the transgender community, as individuals may use pronouns that differ from the ones traditionally associated with their gender identity. Using the correct pronouns is respectful and affirming and can help create a more inclusive and welcoming environment.

Before we get into how to know what someone's pronouns are, let's go over the different pronouns that people may use and how to use them correctly. There are two categories of pronouns to date: Common pronouns and neopronouns.

. . .

Common Pronouns:

- he/him
- she/her
- they/them

Neopronouns:

- xe/xem
- em/eir
- ze/hir
- fae/faer
- Etc.

The common pronouns of he/him and she/her are gendered pronouns that commonly identify someone as either male or female. However, never assume someone's pronouns, even if you know their gender identity. No gender identity has fixed pronouns. Instead, people use pronouns based on what they feel most comfortable with.

If someone's pronouns are "she/her" or "he/his," then you can use them like this:

"Chris went to the beach. He said he'll be back later with his surfboard."

"Jarred is the same age as me, and she also grew up Catholic in her hometown."

They/them has a history of being plural and singular, while the neopronouns have no record of plural usage. For example, both of these sentences are correct usage of they/them:

"That family has a nice boat. They go on vacation often."

"The teacher likes red apples. They eat one every morning in class."

The family is plural; the teacher is singular. In the same way, you could refer to someone as they/them instead of she/her or him/him. For example:

"Amy plays soccer on the field. They love to score goals."

"Timothy can't stand the taste of oatmeal, but their mother makes them eat it anyway."

Even though it may feel strange at first, it is grammatically correct. We only feel strange using they/them for someone we know because we were taught to gender people by how we see them, know them, or by their name.

It might feel tempting to have used "she" for Amy and "he" for Timothy, but that is because we know which binary genders the names Amy and Timothy are generally used for. We are programmed to use gendered pronouns based on this assumption automatically. But, to build an inclusive society, we must change how we use pronouns.

We understand that there are more than two genders in society, and people who fall outside the gender binary suffer when we don't identify them correctly. That can include anyone from cis men who like to wear makeup to trans women who still have some traditionally masculine features.

Neopronouns were created to give trans and non-binary folks the opportunity to find pronouns that more accurately represent their gender identity. Some people don't feel properly reflected by the conventional pronouns of he/him, she/her, or they/them and prefer to use neopronouns.

Neopronouns are used in the same way as traditional pronouns, to refer to a person in the third person (e.g., "Ze went to the store" instead of "She went to the store"). Some individuals may also use neopronouns in the first person to refer to themselves (e.g., "Ze went to the store" instead of "I went to the store").

It is important to note that using neopronouns is a form of self-expression and a way for individuals to affirm their gender identity. Respecting and using an individual's chosen pronouns is crucial to respecting their gender identity and promoting inclusivity and acceptance. It is always best to ask someone what pronouns they prefer and to use them consistently.

It is also possible and common for people of any gender identity to use a combination of pronouns such as "she/they" or "he/they." Using a combination of the two is when someone is comfortable with both "she/her" or "he/him" pronouns AND "they/them" pronouns. However, generally, most transgender people prefer the first pronoun they label themselves with. The second is also acceptable but is an alternative to the first one.

For example, I started my transition using he/him when someone asked what my pronouns were. I chose traditional male pronouns because I didn't understand what being non-binary meant. Once I had more knowledge and understanding, I changed my pronouns to he/they. I'm comfortable with traditional male pronouns but also with being labeled as having no gender at all.

You can think of "they/them" pronouns as "default" pronouns when you aren't sure of someone's pronouns yet. It is a safe option as it does not gender the person you want to discuss.

Changing Gendered Language

Using gendered language goes further in our society than how we address individual people. We hear and use gendered language more than we realize. We do it when we greet strangers, we do it when we address crowds, and we might even do it when addressing children.

Think about the last time you went to watch a live performance or tuned into the radio and heard the presenter say something like, "Good evening, ladies and gentlemen, boys and girls." Instantly the crowd is divided into two basic categories: Men and women. So where does that leave the rest of us?

It is about time that society makes room for all the beautiful people that do not fit into the gender norm. We need to create a new gender norm, one that is inclusive of transgender and non-binary people.

I'm not saying we need to become touchy and aggressive in approaching this, but we can kindly push a new narrative for our emerging community. Gendered language exists to deny us. It is part of the gender binary ideal set up when the LGBTQ+ community was forced to hide in the shadows or face grave consequences. That is the core reason why it has to go.

Inclusive language is part of the change toward a healthier society where everyone can exist, thrive, and enjoy life in harmony. So here are some of the changes that we can make to use inclusive language:

- Replace "ladies and gentlemen" with "everyone" or "folks."
- Replace "you guys" with "you all."
- Stop using words like "dude," "man," or "bro."
- Replace "sir or ma'am" with the person's name.
- Instead of "boys and girls," say "children" or "kids."

As people in the LGBTQ+ community, the change will start with us. Cis-gendered people might not understand right away because using gendered language does not exclude them. But as society grows and we continue to explain why inclusive language is essential, the hope is it will catch on and create a more inclusive world.

.   .   .

The Importance Of Pronouns

According to a 2020 Trevor Project Survey on LGBTQ+ Youth Mental Health, 25% of LGBTQ+ youth use pronouns outside the gender binary, including they/them, a combination of common pronouns, and neopronouns.

The study also showed a 50% decrease in suicide rates among youth who felt their pronouns were respected by most people compared to youth who felt their pronouns were not respected.

This study is an example of just how much of an impact respecting someone's pronouns can have. It's not a matter of being bossed around by people correcting you on their pronouns. Instead, it's fundamentally embracing someone's authentic self and showing them that you respect them.

Feeling respected in society for who someone really is, is what inclusive pronouns are all about. Getting someone's pronouns right is an opportunity to accept their identity and show them you respect them.

Everybody deserves to feel respected, so adding inclusive pronouns to our vocabulary must be a priority. To break it down further, here are five reasons why using correct pronouns is essential:

- To normalize, never assume someone's gender.
- To help trans and non-binary people feel visible.
- To fully respect people and their identities.
- To improve feelings of belonging and acceptance in our society.
- To instill the importance of pronouns as equivalent to getting someone's name right.

You need to know that pronouns are not a choice because using language that implies they are will potentially cause offense in the

LGBTQ+ community. A common way to find out someone's pronouns include saying something like, "Hello, I'm Jane, and my preferred pronouns are she/her. What are your preferred pronouns?" But this is wrong.

Using the word "preferred" implies that someone's pronouns are a matter of preference when they are actually decided upon based on identity.

The correct way to find out what someone's pronouns are is to introduce yourself with your name and pronouns. For example, you can say, "Hi, my name is Braxton. I use he/they pronouns. What about you?"

Keeping your introduction straightforward and stating what your pronouns are opens enough of an opportunity for the person to introduce themselves and express their pronouns in return.

If you have already met someone in the past but can't remember what their pronouns are, you can approach this situation much like you would if you forgot someone's name. For example, you can say, "Hi, I know we've already met, but I'm unsure of your pronouns. Can you please remind me of what they are?"

This can feel embarrassing for many people, so if you are uncomfortable asking someone outright about their pronouns, you can try listening to other people around you addressing the person. You will likely hear someone else use the person's pronouns in passing.

Sometimes we are in a social situation where we are not directly introduced to everyone or want to say something about someone else who isn't present. If you don't know someone's pronouns and they are not around for you to ask, always stick to the pronouns they/them when in doubt. You can use the person's name instead of a pronoun if it makes sense.

· · ·

How To Deal With Mistakes

Be prepared to make mistakes. Learning the pronouns of everyone you know, especially if you encounter many people who use neopronouns, can leave room for mishaps more often than expected. If it happens to you, don't beat yourself up; just deal with the situation as best as possible and move forward.

That said, getting people's pronouns right as much as possible is important. So don't be lazy about it. However, if you do happen to forget someone's pronouns or accidentally use the wrong pronouns, follow these steps to deal with the situation most politely and respectfully:

1. **Don't make a big deal out of it:** Making a big deal about your mistake can lead to more embarrassment for both parties. Sometimes it's best not even to mention the error at all. Move on immediately instead.
2. **Apologize:** With step one in mind, keep your apology to a simple "sorry" before moving ahead with what you meant to say.
3. **Use the correct pronouns:** After briefly acknowledging your mistake, continue with the conversation making an effort to use the correct pronouns.
4. **Embrace pronoun corrections:** If someone corrects you mid-sentence after accidentally using the wrong pronouns, always say "thank you" and use the correct pronouns from then onwards.
5. **Correct others' mistakes:** If you know someone's pronouns and hear another person using the wrong pronouns for them, correct them mid-sentence every time. Don't worry about upsetting someone. It is more important to respect the person being spoken about.
6. **Never make it about you:** It doesn't matter how difficult you find memorizing pronouns. If you make a mistake,

never place your guilt on someone else. It is entirely your responsibility to remember someone else's name and pronouns.

7. **Make an effort, and address your biases:** If you frequently mess up people's pronouns despite knowing their pronouns, you might struggle with embracing trans identities. Get educated on the transgender experience, and talk to a friend or therapist about your view. Being more aware of the importance of pronouns and understanding trans identities will help you use new and different pronouns more easily.

So, if you run into this problem and you want to handle it as respectfully as possible, it would look something like this:

"Michael isn't going to make it to the party. He is feeling sick. Sorry, I meant they are feeling sick."

Or, if you need to correct someone else's mistake, it could look something like this:

You: "Hi Jamie, did you see where Imogen went?"

Friend: "Yes, he went to the soccer field."

You: "She went to the soccer field. She uses she/her pronouns."

Friend: "Thanks! My mistake."

It doesn't have to come across as aggressive or rude to correct someone else's mistake. And you should also try not to be offended when someone corrects you. Fixing incorrect pronouns has nothing to do with you; it is about respecting the other person and their identity.

I made the mistake one Christmas of blowing up on my mom for using incorrect pronouns while telling a story from when I was young. I realized I went about this interaction completely wrong. I should have politely corrected her and should have explained why using correct pronouns, even when talking about me in the past, was so important to me.

The purpose of the chapter is to help readers become good, respectful friends and members of society. The love and inclusivity that we want in society go both ways. Inclusivity means being inclusive of EVERYONE, whether you are in the LGBTQ+ community or not. We need to love and respect each other, despite our differences and understanding of the world. It may not always be easy, but the more we approach change with good intentions and kindness, the faster our message will be accepted.

Transgender and non-binary individuals should deal with their mistakes as kindly as possible. Most people don't mean any harm by their mistake, and being aggressive towards someone paints you in a defensive and unpleasant light. I know this can be difficult and trigger many feelings and potential dysphoria. In order to create a loving and inclusive society, we must reinforce a narrative that is inclusive by using pronouns and gender-neutral language with consistency and respect.

We will discuss how to cope with becoming triggered by someone misgendering you or getting your pronouns wrong in chapters seven and eight of this book. But for now, if you struggle with becoming reactive during these understandably upsetting interactions, start by taking a deep breath before responding with your correction.

And always know that no matter who you are talking to, if you are uncomfortable in the conversation, take a moment for yourself or excuse yourself from the conversation entirely. It is not your responsibility to make other people respect your identity. That is up to them. If they are unwilling to behave appropriately, try not to take it personally and stand firm in who you are.

There are a lot of misconceptions and stereotypes within society trying to disprove and put down the transgender experience. There are even some myths within the LGBTQ+ community that don't serve us, either. So, turn the page to chapter four and debunk some so-called "facts" about being transgender.

4

NAVIGATING GENDER STEREOTYPES

I t is almost impossible to escape myths and misconceptions everywhere in the world. From degrading stereotypes to just general stupidity, if you're looking for misinformation, it's abundant. Sadly, it's the misinformation about the LGBTQ+ community that keeps trans folks of all colors and shades hidden away, denying themselves the right to exist and thrive.

These phony old notions are questioning the nature of transgender people. The pressures and prejudice against being any kind of different in a black-and-white world. And the excuses disguised as evidence, feigning unchangeable bias against our community. The list is endless and will leave you rolling your eyes if you have any sense left.

Let's go over the most common myths and stereotypes about the trans community and bust them to smithereens. Every misconception in this chapter is false, and I'm going to tell you why starting with the myth that being trans is a choice.

Being Transgender Is A Choice

I understand why some people might get the impression that being transgender is a choice, especially when seeing someone you know suddenly transition away from the gender you've always assumed them to be.

Transgender individuals do not choose to feel like their gender identity does not match their biological sex, just as cisgender individuals (those who identify with their assigned sex at birth) do not choose to identify with their gender.

From the outside looking, it isn't always apparent that someone may not identify with their assigned gender. I get it. If you aren't in that person's shoes, it certainly can seem like some unexpected choice or phase the person is going through out of the blue. But the truth is, transgender people are transgender from birth. It is a biological difference in the person's brain and genetic makeup.

We've already discussed the studies to prove how trans brains physically resemble the gender they identify with in chapter one. But even before this study was released, psychologists and medical professionals have agreed for some time that being transgender is an innate quality influenced mainly by biology.

Transgender individuals often experience gender dysphoria, a clinically recognized condition in which there is a disconnect between their gender identity and their biological sex, making them feel uncomfortable. This can cause significant distress and discomfort, causing many transgender individuals to feel compelled to transition to live as their true selves.

While studies are limited, there is more than enough evidence to prove the innate factors that create the transgender experience. But above all, it is vital to listen to and consider the real-life experiences of the trans community.

. . .

Children Don't Understand Their Own Gender

The myth that children don't understand their gender is just that—a myth. Children often have a strong sense of their gender identity from a young age.

From the time I was three years old, I was checking every box that your typical cisgendered little boy would. I wore backward caps and baggy clothes and dreamed of becoming a firefighter one day—nothing you wouldn't expect until you considered my assigned gender: female. While most little girls with loving mothers were out there messing in their mommy's makeup bag and picking up on her mannerisms, I only had eyes for my dad.

I didn't feel like a girl with "boyish" tendencies. I *knew* I was a boy and felt comfortable in my own skin. That is until I was told over and over again that I'm a girl and taught all the things girls are "supposed" to do. Yes, I became confused about my gender, but only after I was pushed into the gender binary box of penis, meaning boy, and vagina, meaning girl—no exceptions.

My point is children can and do comprehend gender. It starts with identifying physical differences between the sexes around age two. Then, by the age of three, most children are able to identify and label themselves as either a "boy" or "girl." And by the age of four, most children have a more in depth grasp of their gender identity, including many trans and non-binary kids.

Research has also shown that children who identify as transgender or gender non-conforming often have a deep and persistent sense of their gender identity, even at a very young age. Studies have found that transgender children are as sure about their gender identity as their cisgender peers.

Whether a child's gender identity aligns with societal expectations or not, supporting and affirming them is crucial. This can help them develop a positive self-image and reduce the risk of mental health issues later in life. Conversely, rejecting or denying a child's gender identity can harm their emotional well-being and increase anxiety, depression, and suicide.

A study I found interesting that supports this notion is "Gender Diversity in Young Children: A Longitudinal Study of Identity, Expression, and Perception" by Olson, K. R., Durwood, L., DeMeules, M., & McLaughlin, K. A. (2016). This study focused on the gender diversity of young children and examined the mental health outcomes associated with supportive environments for transgender children.

The researchers followed a group of 73 transgender children aged 3 to 12 for three years, comparing their mental health outcomes to those of cisgender (non-transgender) children and transgender children who did not receive support for their gender identity. The study utilized various measures, including self-reporting by children and parental assessments.

The mental health outcomes of children supported in their gender identities were similar to those of their cisgender peers. These children exhibited levels of depression and anxiety that were no higher than those of their cisgender counterparts. In contrast, transgender children who did not receive support for their gender identity had significantly higher levels of depression and anxiety.

Importantly, this study provides empirical evidence supporting the positive impact of gender-affirming environments on the mental well-being of transgender children. Furthermore, it demonstrates that embracing gender diversity and supporting children's gender identities can contribute to healthier outcomes in terms of mental health.

Gender may seem like something too complex for children to understand, but whether we talk about gender or not, children have a natural inclination to understand their own gender as well as the genders of the people around them. It's time our society becomes more educated on this so that we can open space for trans and non-binary kids to express their true identities and feel normal in how they identify.

Gender Diversity Is Not A Topic For Children

Children begin to develop their gender identities at a young age, and they need to understand that gender is a spectrum and not limited to binary options.

By ignoring gender diversity, we risk perpetuating harmful stereo-types and limiting children's understanding of themselves and others. It's important to expose children to diverse representations of gender, including non-binary and gender-nonconforming individuals, to foster a more inclusive and accepting society.

With children being able to identify themselves as either a boy or a girl by the age of three, it presses the issue that gender diversity is indeed a topic meant for children. As many parents would like to think that gender is only something kids worry about after puberty, understanding gender identity is crucial to a child's overall identity and well-being.

We don't put off educating children about other subjects we feel are too advanced for them, like reproductive organs, kidnapping, and death, so why do we tip-toe around the topic of gender diversity when kids are experiencing it from the age of three? If children are old enough to be told that they are a girl even if they feel like a boy, and vice versa, then they are old enough to be told that there are people who experience no gender, different genders than what they were assigned, or multiple genders.

Like any other difficult subject to discuss with children, there are appropriate ways and appropriate times when educating your child about gender diversity. If we fail to do so, we fail our children by setting them up for confusion within their identity if they don't fit the binary construct.

I knew I didn't fit into the binary boxes we were taught, but I wasn't open to asking my parents about it. The topic of gender diversity felt taboo to me—it was something that felt very uncomfortable to discuss. Most people around me chose not to mention anything about it to me at all.

A prime example is when 12-year-old me had to stand as a junior bridesmaid for my Aunt B's wedding. We were all in Downtown Cleveland, having pictures taken by the Rock n' Roll hall of fame around the same time the annual Pride Parade took place. Seeing the bright colors and smiling faces coming down the street as laughter and joy filled the air, I couldn't be more intrigued. But nothing about the parade or what it was for was ever mentioned to me. I only know now, looking back, what it meant. I was left out of the loop about gender diversity, which cost me. If I had been properly educated about it, I know things would have been different. Maybe I wouldn't have been so hard on myself for not fitting in and simply embraced my identity as it was.

All children deserve to understand that gender is not binary and that gender differences exist. Discussing gender diversity with children in an appropriate way not only helps trans kids better identify them-selves from the same ages as their peers, but it also takes away the notion that being anything but a cis boy or a girl is different or "weird."

If children understand that it is normal for some kids to identify as a different gender than what they were assigned or to identify as no gender, they will be more likely to embrace their gender-diverse peers without bullying them or seeing them as anything unusual.

Furthermore, studies have shown that children who learn about gender diversity at a young age are more likely to be empathetic and accepting of others.

Real Transgender People Know They're Trans As Children

Before we move on, I want to clarify that not all transgender people know their true gender identity from childhood. This is a big misconception invalidating the experience of many people in the LGBTQ+ community.

Yes, many trans people experience some sense of gender dysphoria or feelings of being "different," but that doesn't mean that you *need* to know you're trans from adolescence to be considered valid in your experience. Many trans people only discover their gender diversity after puberty or well into adulthood.

There are many reasons for this, from trans kids being forced into binary ideals from a young age and gaslighted about their true experiences, to people only feeling comfortable exploring their identity as an adult. Whatever the reason is, it's there, and it's valid.

Conversations with children about gender diversity from a young age will help many gender-diverse people understand themselves better from childhood. However, it is still possible to only discover your true identity later in life, even if you grew up educated about gender.

It is also possible for anyone to identify differently at different stages in their life. Although it is considered rare by doctors and psychologists specializing in the trans experience, even cisgender people can grow to have a more fluid identity. It's a controversial topic in society as a whole, whether or not someone's identity can truly shift in this way, with many arguing that people having this experience were trans all along. But this is not necessarily the case; many people have experienced a gender identity shift later in life.

Before jumping to conclusions or forming our own biases about specific experiences within the gender diversity space, it is crucial to always listen to real experiences and take those experiences seriously, whether they go with your ideals or not. We are all humans with beating hearts and blood pumping through our veins. It's time we embrace differences as the natural occurrences that they are and stop invalidating trans experiences out of our biased opinions.

Transgender People Are Confused Or Mentally Ill

As we're discussing transgender experiences and how people can jump to conclusions about experiences they don't understand, this myth is a painfully common one—that transgender people are only confused about their gender or that they are suffering from mental illness.

As a kid, I was super social, happy-go-lucky, and bubbly. I was confident in myself and found no difficulty accepting who I was or loving myself. I was not born with any type of mental illness or an unknown predisposition to one. But as I grew older and felt the pressures and prods of society telling me what and who I should be, a shadow of doubt was cast over my bright personality.

My mental health began to decline without being able to embrace my true identity and express that to the world in the way I wanted to. My grades slipped, I became distracted by hiding my diverse identity beneath a shell of deceit, and I even contemplated self-injury on multiple occasions. I fell into a deep pit of darkness–a darkness I told myself I would never let myself feel. This was all because of environmental factors and had nothing to do with my innate qualities or because I'm transgender.

While discovering you're trans or non-binary can be a confusing experience, trying to be your most authentic self and figuring out who that is, doesn't mean you're confused about being gender diverse. Most gender-diverse people are certain that they are different in some way and that they do not fit the binary gender norms.

The American Psychological Association, the World Health Organization, and other major medical and mental health organizations have all recognized that being transgender is not a mental disorder. While some transgender people may experience mental health challenges like anxiety or depression, these issues are often a result of social stigma, discrimination, and lack of acceptance rather than being inherent to being transgender.

It is also worth understanding that just because an experience is difficult or confusing doesn't mean it isn't a valid experience. In many ways, the difficulty of the trans experience comes from a lack of understanding from other people and society rather than from within. I believe the trans and non-binary experience would be much easier for people to embrace and accept within themselves if society was already gender inclusive.

Just like society and its stereotypes are a large cause for difficulty and confusion within the trans experience, an society not inclusive is often why trans and other LGBTQ+ people experience mental illnesses such as depression and anxiety.

Think about how I could go from my innate, happy self to wanting to physically harm myself. In the same way, many other trans people suffer the consequence of society's tight boundaries of who can and can't exist in our diverse world. Although mental illness can be genetic, it is not an innate part of the trans experience; much of it is provoked by a society that doesn't embrace diversity.

Trans And Non-Binary People Can Never Be Truly Happy

I have a ways to go as far as being 100% happy, but not because of who I am or my decisions. It's because I still have to fight for my own existence in this world. I'm not proud of every decision I've made, especially those before transitioning. i.e., lying all the time, doing drugs, and drinking recklessly.

Even after starting my transition, I've made some really stupid mistakes that have brought me some unhappiness. But moving on and letting go of my mistakes has allowed me to feel a happiness I never thought I could. I've surrounded myself with people who truly care and I participate in activities I truly enjoy. Focusing on the people and things that bring me authentic happiness has been the key to my success.

You can do many things to cultivate true happiness in your life, but a great place to start is to forgive yourself for your mistakes and accept that not everyone will love your transition. Here are more things you can do:

- **Accept yourself:** This means acknowledging your gender identity and being comfortable with it. How can you expect others to accept and love you if you can't accept and love yourself?
- **Find support:** A good support system goes a very long way. You can find support in the form of friends, family, and trans communities either in person or online. You can also contact support groups, try therapy, or join online forums.
- **Live your truth:** Living authentically and expressing your true self is a powerful source of happiness. This can mean changing your name, pronouns, and gender expression to match your gender identity.
- **Create a safe and affirming environment:** Spend time in places where the people around you are accepting and open to gender diversity. You can create this environment for yourself at work, school, and at home by

surrounding yourself with people who love you and respect your differences.

- **Pursue your hobbies and interests:** Fill your life with the activities and hobbies that bring you the most joy. Sometimes we get caught up in our everyday struggles, but doing things you love can make you feel more present.
- **Transition medically:** Don't be afraid to start transitioning medically if it will make you feel more fulfilled and happy. This can include hormone therapy and surgeries. Many trans folks feel their quality of life improves drastically when their bodies reflect how they see themselves inside.

The path to finding happiness for transgender people is unique and varies from person to person. The most important thing you can do is find what works best for you and live as authentically as possible. Be true to yourself, and don't let anyone tell you you're doomed to be unhappy. It's simply not true. Trans people are no more or less capable of living a happy life than anybody else.

I'll be the first to admit that the journey of self-discovery and self-acceptance is not always easy. But, trans or not, it rarely is. That is why learning to love yourself and embrace your diversity is one of the most important things you can do to find happiness and fulfillment in life.

It's also no mystery why being trans might come with more challenges. We live in a society where we have to fight for trans rights and go through things that most cis people don't, like transitioning or risking judgment when coming out to family and friends. But that doesn't mean there isn't room for us to live an amazing life.

We are arguably some of the happiest people alive once we come to terms with transitioning. Not only can we embrace and love ourselves in a world that tells us it shouldn't be possible, but we know how to embrace and love others for who they truly are. That's *true* happiness.

Transgender People All Transition Medically

With modern medicine able to do incredible things, it's become a hot topic in gender diversity to discuss transitioning from a medical standpoint. This includes hormone therapy, gender reassignment surgery, and general cosmetic surgeries. But just because you can transition medically, doesn't mean you have to; and sometimes you may want to but won't be able to.

How you express your gender identity doesn't make you more or less trans. Being trans is something you already are; transitioning is only a way to express yourself and feel more authentic in your identity and gender expression.

Before I transitioned, I was already pretty happy with my appearance, besides a few feminine features and voice. However, I still decided to transition medically, taking hormone replacement therapy, because I was labeled as female by those around me based on my few feminine qualities.

I'm trying not to let society govern how much more I do to transition, but I have considered getting top surgery too. Maybe it will be something I do in the future, but nothing's set in stone. I will make that decision when I'm ready to, and if I can see it drastically improving the dysphoria I experience.

It's worth noting that while I am privileged enough to be on hormone replacement therapy, not everyone who wants to can. Some people are allergic to hormone therapy, and others have medical conditions standing in their way. Everyone's experience will be completely unique, yet valid.

You can come out as trans and not change anything about yourself or do whatever medical treatments you feel necessary. Transitioning is very personal and private and should not be something you feel pressured into doing to feel valid in your trans experience.

Many people in the trans community choose to love and embrace their bodies as they are, while others benefit from medically transitioning. But medically transitioning is not the only way to transition as a gender-diverse person. There are many non-medical ways you can express your gender identity.

From hair, clothing, and mannerisms, to changing your pronouns or name, you can have fun rediscovering your true identity and express yourself in whichever way brings you the most happiness.

It Only Takes One Simple Surgery To Transition

The transition process for a transgender person is much more than just getting one simple surgery. A full transition doesn't always involve any surgery at all. A person's transition starts the moment that person feels ready to accept their gender identity and start expressing it to the world.

Transitioning as a trans person is a multi-faceted process. It can involve a complex range of medical, social, and legal procedures. Surgery is a part of medical transitioning, but it is not the only option, and it is not always necessary.

Medical transitioning often includes hormone therapy to help with physical changes in the body such as testosterone to help deepen the voice and grow facial hair, and estrogen to grow breast tissue. Surgeries are also a part of a medical transition, including chest reconstruction, genital reconstruction, and facial feminization or masculinization. Each person doing a medical transition will have a unique experience and may or may not include some or all of these procedures.

In addition to a medical transition, social and legal transitioning steps are also important to take along this journey. A trans person may choose to change their name and change their gender marker on legal documents. Part of this process includes coming out to friends and family, changing pronouns, and finding inclusion at work or other social environments.

Many people don't realize that gender-reassignment surgery is a very big procedure requiring ongoing medical care and potential follow-up surgeries.

Many trans people feel it is important to go through with this surgery to feel more authentically themselves in their physical body. Still, many others are not comfortable with the idea at all. There is no right or wrong in this decision, as your physical sex does not indicate your gender identity.

A surgical transition is generally not the first thing people consider when beginning a transition on their journey because there are so many factors that come before such a surgery.

Another thing to note is transitioning can be as long or as short of a process as you like, but if you choose a medical or surgical approach, it will likely be a much longer and more physically intensive process. This is not meant to scare you or put you off of a medical transition, but knowing how seriously you need to take this approach and what to expect is important.

A very wise trans woman I met a few years ago at the LGBT Center of Greater Cleveland told me something that has resonated with me since I started my transition almost four years ago. She told me to treat my transition as if it were a casserole needing to be cooked from the inside out. You can't microwave the meal and expect to have a warm center by the end of it. But, by sticking it in the oven, cooking it slowly, and at a low temperature, that casserole will come out crispy, golden, and with a warm center.

I use this analogy to reiterate the point that a person's transition is crucial, and it is important to take the process on your own terms and to take it slowly. Transgender people may feel a strong sense of urgency to transition due to the discomfort and dysphoria they experience with their gender identity. While it is understandable to want to transition as quickly as possible, rushing the process can harm their physical, emotional, and social well-being.

The Trans Community Has A Harmful Agenda

As gender diversity has become a more widely accepted and understood topic, it is no surprise that there is more openly trans youth today than there were a generation or two ago. Unfortunately, since the inclusion of gender diversity in the school education curriculum across the US and other countries, some groups and many parents are opposed to the change.

With more youth feeling comfortable enough in modern society to come out as trans and embrace a transition at younger ages than ever before, medical transitioning is another heated topic of discussion that has come to light.

While medically transitioning comes with its pros and cons, for many trans youth it is a matter of life and death. Nonetheless, the controversy surrounding the topic of medical transitions in children and teens has caused some people to assume that the trans community is trying to spread a harmful agenda on children and society.

The only "agenda" that comes from the trans community is to raise awareness and acceptance of gender diversity, to open up an environment where children can be themselves and embrace who they are before they fall into needless depression or experience anxiety due to a lack of sense of belonging within society.

Being Transgender Is A New Trend

We've seen a massive rise in transgender people outwardly expressing their gender diversity in recent years, with 1.4% of 13-17-year-olds identifying as trans in the US, while only 0.5% of adults above 25 are openly trans. And although it seems like trans people are coming out of nowhere to anyone outside the LGBTQ+ community, according to trans history, we've been around as long as people have been able to take note of it.

The furthest reference to gender diversity goes as far back as the copper age to a five-thousand-year-old transgender skeleton. The skeleton, found in the Czech Republic, was sexed as male but strictly buried in the same way as female skeletons. According to specialists, ancient cultures with strict burial rituals would never make a mistake. So it is theorized that the person whose skeleton was found had to have been socially accepted as a woman, despite being born male.

There are references to more than two genders almost everywhere worldwide for thousands of years. Some of the countries and cultures that have long since continued to embrace gender diversity include:

- Africa
- Asia
- Pacific Islands
- Catholic Italy
- Native America

Across these cultures, many have identified and accepted a "third" gender within society, with others seeing gender-diverse people as good luck and even religiously celebrated. This shows how the trans community in western culture is jeopardized by not embracing gender diversity and fluidity. It is a natural part of human culture and society, so to deny gender diversity is to deny human rights—plain and simple.

Science Is Transphobic

Maybe while discussing basic high-school biology, science can seem transphobic. Topics like genital anatomy between men and women, sex-determining chromosomes, and pubescent hormones like estrogen and testosterone—the science certainly *seems* binary.

While there may be individual scientists who hold discriminatory beliefs, the scientific community as a whole is committed to objectivity, accuracy, and inclusivity.

In fact, scientific research has played a crucial role in advancing our understanding of gender identity and transgender experiences. For example, neuroimaging studies have shown that the brains of transgender individuals may have structural and functional differences compared to cisgender individuals. This research has helped to destigmatize transgender identities and promote greater acceptance and understanding.

Chimerism is a condition in which an individual has two distinct sets of cells with different genetic makeups. In the case of 46,XX/46,XY chimerism, an individual may have both XX and XY cell lines in their body. The presence of both male and female cell lines can result in variations in reproductive organs, external genitalia, and hormone levels. Gender identity can vary in individuals with chimerism and may not necessarily align with their assigned sex at birth. It's important to remember that while these chromosomal variations may have physical and physiological implications, they do not directly determine an individual's gender identity.

In addition to neuroimaging and chromosomal variations, genetic factors can contribute to variations in sexual development and anatomy. For example, mutations in genes involved in sexual development, such as the androgen receptor gene, can lead to atypical development and variations in gender-related traits. These genetic variations highlight the complexity and diversity within human biology.

It's only when you dig a little deeper and explore more advanced explanations of each of these gender-confirming biological processes that you start to notice how scientific gender diversity is. Every aspect of sex and gender in humans points towards the possibility and likelihood of gender-diverse people.

An unexpected example that might blow your mind, is the fact that someone who is born with XX chromosomes, the supposed determining factor of females, can also be born with a complete set of gonads. It happens, and it happens more often than you might think.

We've already discussed the biology of intersex people and differences in trans brains in chapter one. But just to reiterate: Being transgender is biological. From differences in brain structure, pubescent hormones, and innate behavior, it is clear that gender diversity is entirely natural.

After busting all these myths and misconceptions about the trans community, I hope you feel more validated in your experience or understand the trans experience better. However, it doesn't end there. How people treat the trans community is just as important as understanding and accepting gender diversity.

Part of the problem with misinformation and a lack of understanding is people saying hurtful things or asking inappropriate questions to trans people. So, to end off this chapter with a bang, here are ten stereotypical things you should NEVER say to a transgender person and why.

10 Things To Never Say To A Trans Person

1. **You've obviously had "the operation." What is it like having a fake vagina/penis:** Asking a transgender person about the intimate details of their body is invasive, disrespectful, and hurtful, especially if your question invalidates the authenticity of their experience or physical body. It is also inappropriate to make assumptions about what medical procedures someone has had during their transition or otherwise.

2. **Are you a man or a woman?** Asking this implies that there are only two binary genders and assumes that gender is easily determined by someone's appearance or external factors, which is not the case. Therefore, this question invalidates and denies someone's gender identity. You should respect someone's pronouns and gender identity regardless of their appearance.

3. **I know you identify as male/female, but do you have a penis or a vagina?** Transgender people may or may not choose to undergo gender reassignment surgeries during their transition. But, whether they do or not, genitals do not determine someone's gender identity or expression. Not only is it invasive, it is invalidating and denying the gender identity of the person.

4. **Why did you go trans? Are you *sure* you're not just confused?** This question implies that being transgender is a choice or a phase that is untrue and will deny or negate someone's gender identity. Gender identity is a core aspect of a person's identity for both cis and trans people, so disrespecting it can cause significant distress and discomfort.

5. **I want to see what you looked like before. Can I see a picture?** Many trans people may have experienced significant trauma, discrimination, or harassment before or during their transition. Asking to see a picture from before is invasive and can bring up painful memories or emotions for someone. Some people are comfortable showing old photos, however, if they don't initiate the interaction it is still inappropriate to ask.

6. **So, what's your real name?** Transgender people often choose a new name that reflects their gender identity, which is just as authentic and valid as their birth name. Asking what someone's "real" name implies that their chosen name is invalid. Always use a person's chosen name to respect their gender identity and acknowledge their experience.

7. **I would never tell that you're trans. You look cis.** I get this one a lot. You might think it's a compliment, but this statement implies that being transgender is something to be ashamed about or best kept hidden—this is not true. Trans folks should not be pressured to conform to gender norms or try to hide their identity and "pass" as cisgender to feel accepted and valid.

8. **I support your transition, but it's hard for me to use your pronouns.** Using incorrect pronouns can make a person feel disrespected and invalidated, contributing to their feelings of dysphoria and discomfort. Refusing to use someone's pronouns shows that you don't respect or understand why their pronouns are important to them. Try to prioritize the needs and feelings of the transgender person over your own challenges with using pronouns.

9. **Remind me of when you decided to be transgender?** This question assumes that being transgender is a choice or a decision someone makes, which is untrue. Being transgender is integral to one's identity.

10. **You're so attractive for a trans person!** This comment is downright disrespectful, even if you think you're giving a compliment. Saying this implies that transgender people are inherently not attractive, which is entirely false. A person's attractiveness should not be based on their gender identity. It is important to treat all people with respect and dignity, regardless of their gender identity or physical characteristics.

Overall, it is essential to remember that transgender individuals should be treated with the same respect and dignity as anyone else. This includes using their name and pronouns, respecting their boundaries, and avoiding making insensitive or invalidating statements about their gender identity.

I think it goes without saying that any of the above should never be said to a transgender person. When you address trans people, it's crucial to think about what you say and make sure you aren't putting their identity down, invalidating their experience, or being inappropriate.

Many of these topics are up to the individual to disclose or talk about. And, most likely, they will only ever open up to close friends, family, and romantic partners about specific details. Other details, however, are generally kept between them and their doctors or sexual partners.

Now, on the topic of relationships. Turn to chapter five, where we go through the social implications of disclosing your gender diversity to the people around you and how to surround yourself with the best support system you can get.

PLEASE LEAVE A
REVIEW

Enjoying the book so far? By sharing your thoughts, experiences, and recommendations, you contribute to a more inclusive and supportive environment for all.

5

GENDER IN RELATIONSHIPS

After coming to terms with who I am, I felt a sense of relief clouded by fear. I knew that the journey ahead of me would not be easy, even though I knew little about why. I had just faced my first hurdle—while you focus your energy on healing, embracing your trans identity, and becoming your most authentic self, you may face adversity in almost every area of your life.

This chapter is here to prepare you for the worst and empower you to know that you will handle whatever happens as best as possible. You don't need to do more or be better. Instead, focus on your well-being for now and mend the relationships that matter when you're ready. Your relationship with yourself is your priority.

Even though I was living with my girlfriend then, my confidence in who I was felt low. I wasn't sure how my identity reveal would affect our relationship, and I wasn't ready to find out. So I pretended like nothing had changed. Hiding that monumental shift within me seemed contradictory, but it was all I could think to do.

It wasn't long before I felt urged to tell someone, and I knew exactly who I needed that to be. So one evening, I decided to visit the campgrounds in Pennsylvania where my parents, aunt, and uncle all camp for the summer. Their campers were close enough to each other to make a fire and spend time together but far enough apart that I could get a moment alone with my aunt Margie.

Watching the flames crackle and flare, I felt zoned out momentarily. Then, my mind went wild, wondering where to start and how to go about this conversation. Aunt Margie was sipping her drink, sitting laid-back on her camping chair as she admired the quiet sunset.

"What's on your mind, darling?" she asked.

I didn't know how to answer, but somehow words just started flying out of my mouth in a satisfying stream of release. Although I was nervous about my aunt's reaction, the relief I felt overpowered any fear I had at that moment; the comfort and the fact that I trusted she might understand. Then I went quiet.

She smiled. And I know I'm lucky for this because not everyone is met with such acceptance their first time coming out. But her smile that afternoon was one I'll never forget. She smiled and quickly told me it would be okay before beckoning me in for a hug. We agreed to keep it between us until I was ready to open up more. It started a painful yet beautiful journey toward where I am today, living my authentic life.

Things were still a mess, and I hadn't come out to anyone else yet. Life seemed to drag me along like a rag doll—I did all the everyday things, but the energy behind my eyes seemed to fade the longer I went on without living my truth. Another year went by.

My girlfriend and I broke up fall of 2018, and we moved apart. When I finally came out to her, I could tell she wasn't thrilled by her reaction and what she said. Unfortunately, the statement she made has stuck with me until this day, but it has been the fuel to my fire.

When I finally started my transition, I still maintained a consistent, low-grade resistance to the truth. I was unhappy. Then, one day during the summer, I was visiting my mom, and something came over me again, like that night around the campfire with Aunt Margie, but much less controlled. While my mom was grabbing a diet Pepsi from the fridge in her camper's kitchen, I stood nearby, engaging in our everyday small talk. My stomach felt tight as the truth ate away at me.

Suddenly, I couldn't hold it in anymore. The small talk quickly turned into my confession. It was a confession I knew my mom might not react well to, but there's something about hiding a part of you from your mother that kills you inside. So I let it all out and waited for her reaction.

My mom's reaction wasn't how I dreamed it could be, but it wasn't the worst. I still remember how it made me feel, but through the pain of not being understood, I felt relieved. I thought that if my mom knew and could accept it in some way, then I could finally be free and start opening up to the world. Not long after this, I joined the LGBT Center of Greater Cleveland and started attending support groups up to three times per week to help me further understand and accept my identity.

After a few months of meeting like-minded people, people who accepted and embraced my diversity almost instantly, I began to feel the most comfortable in my skin than ever before. I felt the most authentic me I'd been since my Mickey-Mouse t-shirt-wearing days. I felt the most free.

So, after much deliberation, a couple of months later, on my birthday, I decided that I was finally going to stop looking to others for approval and come out publicly. I changed my name and pronouns on Facebook and started living life as the real me: Braxton Phoenix Stock. I knew that too much was at stake to let one more person or opinion stand in my way of becoming my most authentic self. Most of my family was unsupportive, but for the first time, I just didn't care.

Like ripping off a bandaid, I chose to come out quickly and publicly from that point onward before something, or someone could convince me otherwise. I still thank myself for the bravery I was able to pull together back then because now I can focus on the things that matter in life rather than going around in circles denying myself the life I deserve. I can feel comfortable in my identity and live as best I can. I can start to live a life of happiness.

The thing about identity is it plays a role in our position in society. Our expression, behavior, and social groups reflect what we believe about ourselves on the outside, which helps people identify with us. The trouble with gender identity is that it isn't always outwardly expressed as expected. That's where "coming out" is often necessary.

Once you have embraced your true authentic self, sharing your identity with others is essential to stay socially healthy. It can almost feel deceptive if you don't feel like you are being or expressing your authentic self with the people you love. You won't feel as fulfilled or understood either because the person they know isn't who you are.

I won't deny that coming out is scary. I also can't promise that everyone will love and accept you as you are. But what I can promise is that everyone who matters will. Healthy relationships with family, friends, or partners are some of the most important dynamics for a happy life, trans or not.

The trouble with relationships for trans people is that many of the relationships you may build before coming out or transitioning will be with people who are only prepared to know and love you the way you were and not how you indeed are. But before you feel like you can't make this vital change for yourself, I want you to pause for a moment and find any sense of bravery you have within you.

Maybe life is passing you by without any significant highs or lows, or perhaps you're caught in a depression, grasping for a way out like I was. Either way, I want you to consider why living authentically is of the utmost importance. Don't think about what anyone else might think.

Just like it was for me, I can imagine that hiding your truth has been painful. So maybe you're reading this book to find the validation you need to send you on your way and live the life you deserve. Or perhaps you were given this book to help you understand your trans journey better. Whatever the reason is that made you pick up this book and get this far into it, think about that and don't let anything stand in your way moving forward.

Coming out about your trans identity is not something you need to feel pressured to do right away. You can take as long as you need to and do it in as many small increments as you want. For example, you can choose to tell only one person or work your way up to a social media reveal. Whatever's the most comfortable and suitable for you, I encourage you to think about it and take as much time as you need.

To help you along, I will use the rest of this chapter to discuss the different types of relationships you will likely encounter on your journey, why they are important, and how you can best navigate them after coming out or transitioning.

While we build a more inclusive society, we need to create a support system. A support system can consist of friends, family, your community, and more, but it is not limited. Your support system can be as big or as small as you need it to be, with smaller support systems often being just as effective as bigger ones.

It's also important to know that biological family doesn't necessarily need to form part of your support system. As long as your relationships with your supportive circle are healthy and full of love, it doesn't matter who they are.

. . .

Family

Families are often depicted as the people in your life that you live with and have been a part of your life since childhood. The typical picture of a happy family in society is a mom and a dad with their children. However, diverse families are valid, dysfunctional families are common, and people that are not blood-related can still be family. That said, there are two types of families that you can turn to for support:

- **Biological:** This is any family that you are blood-related to. It can include parents, siblings, aunts, uncles, etc.
- **Chosen:** This is anyone you have selected to be a part of your family. It can include anyone from your biological family, friends, or other people you have a strong relationship with who are not biologically related to you.

You should know that you do not need to feel obligated to have someone in your support system that is harmful to your mental health just because they are blood family. If they are not reliable or understanding, don't try to rely on them in your times of need. Often, this is where your chosen family comes into play.

Of course, suppose you have a healthy connection with your biological family unit, as I have with my two sisters. In that case, that doesn't mean you won't benefit from creating a chosen family unit, especially as an adult living away from home. It can include close friends or even roommates and work colleagues. Anyone you can trust enough to be vulnerable with and who is an active part of your life can form part of your chosen family.

While my experience with having an unsupportive family has been challenging, I must add that this experience is not unique. Unfortunately, it is prevalent for people sharing their trans identity to lose family, friends, and partners. And although it's often best at the end of the day, it's something to keep in mind and prepare for.

What I mean by losing family can include:

- **Parents disowning their children:** This is a harrowing and traumatic event that should not be taken lightly. It can happen if parents have radical belief systems or don't understand and feel overwhelmed by the information. They may be unequipped to handle the situation correctly and react poorly for lack of knowing better.
- **Family cutting contact:** Family members the person may have been close to that are not in their immediate family may choose to cut contact out of a lack of understanding, a sense of loss for the person they knew, or a radical belief system.
- **Cutting contact with family:** If a family member is not accepting, is abusive, or is generally causing harm, cutting ties with them is an option for the person coming out.

There are many reasons why trans people coming out may lose family members. For example, some family members might cut ties to control the situation or deal with their pain and bias. Or, the trans person may focus on building a chosen family rather than wasting time on toxic relationship dynamics with the biological family.

It is also a sad reality that 40% of homeless youth in the US identify as LGBTQ+. With LGBTQ+ youth making up only 7% of the population, that is a shocking and painful statistic. The reasons for homelessness amongst LGBTQ+ youth vary from violence in the home to sexual abuse. But most commonly, it is simply due to a lack of acceptance and understanding.

I know this is painful to hear, especially if you are considering coming out to your family and are scared about the consequences. However, I don't want to hide any unfortunate truths from you to protect you from the pain. Losing family, friends, and partners is possible; you should be prepared for it.

But I want you to know that no matter what happens, I am here for you, as is the majority of the LGBTQ+ community. No matter where you go or who you are, people will be willing to accept and understand you exactly how you are and will be willing to grow as you do. The world is a prominent place, and our community is only growing and reaching the light more and more. So don't let fear hold you back. Be prepared for the worst, but by all means, hope for the best.

Friends

Along your coming out journey and transition, you may find that the friends you make will be your biggest supporters. Therefore, I encourage you to prioritize finding like-minded friends when building your support system.

Friends are invaluable because they are people you choose to have in your life. They are not there out of obligation but because they *want* to be there, and you want them there. They may even become part of your chosen family.

When I first came out publicly, I wasn't prepared for my transition's effect on my social circle. I lost one of my closest and oldest friends, a friend I'd had for ten years. Unfortunately, some mistakes I made at the beginning of my transition were too much. Other friends had a hard time adjusting to my new identity.

The beginning of my journey was pretty lonely. I didn't expect the fallouts that happened to happen because I wasn't prepared. But once I joined an LGBTQ+ support group and felt the love and acceptance of true friends, I only wished that I felt that love sooner.

That is why you must prioritize making new, like-minded friends over trying to mend friendships with people who might never understand. Don't waste your time trying to pry acceptance out of people when friends are willing to accept you instantly. Making new friends is easier than it seems, and I'm going to show you how.

- **Let go of preconceived notions:** Before opening yourself up to new friends from the trans and LGBTQ+ community, you must let go of old or mistaken beliefs regarding what these friends might look like or where they might hang out. You can make like-minded friends by doing activities you enjoy.
- **Search for local activity groups and meet-ups:** There are plenty of groups and meet-ups specifically for LGBTQ+ people. Research and look for activity groups for LGBTQ+ people in your area. Groups you could join include sports teams, art classes, and many other activities where people can come together and meet like-minded friends in a safe and fun environment.
- **Sign up for online chat groups and forums:** On almost every social media or meet-up platform, you will find chat groups and forums for LGBTQ+ communities. Try joining Facebook groups or signing up for trans-centered meet-ups on platforms like Discord and Zoom. Practice caution; there will always be spam and fake accounts in any online group, but have fun!
- **Follow trans and LGBTQ+ hashtags:** You don't always have to meet people in your town to make valuable connections. A great start to feeling more accepted is to follow hashtags related to your experience. You will not only find some great and relatable content, but you might

even make a friend if you decide to engage with an account.

- **Experience the queer club scene:** If you're open to a night out or testing a new setting, be open-minded and head to a gay bar. Many LGBTQ+ people, including trans people, enjoy spending time at gay bars. So long as you're not recovering from drinking or drug abuse, gay bars are a fun and exciting option to make new friends.
- **Attend live performances:** Another place where you will find many like-minded LGBTQ+ people is a live performance centered around the community, particularly drag shows and stand-up comedy. If you're unsure, don't hesitate to call or email ahead to learn more.
- **Just live your life:** Once you come out and start living more authentically, you might find that other like-minded people naturally begin to see you! Everyone has to run day-to-day errands and engage in activities they enjoy; it's no different for trans folks. You will attract the right people into your life over time by simply living your life as a more authentic one.

The most important advice I can give regarding making new friends is to be yourself and be patient. Making friends isn't always easy or natural. Sometimes it takes a little persistence and effort. But as long as you're authentically you, you will attract the friends you've been hoping for.

For example, if you join an art class for LGBTQ+ people, don't just go once and never return because you may feel awkward. Instead, keep returning at least a couple of times, prioritize enjoying yourself, and watch how you grow with the people around you.

You can feel assured knowing that your true friends love the *real* you. There's no pretending, hiding, or feeling fake. You can be yourself and know that you are loved and accepted for who you truly are.

. . .

Community

One of the most valuable forms of support for marginalized groups, such as the trans community, is finding a safe space to share, be understood, and feel connected. The value of these connections is why it's so important for LGBTQ+ people to unite in a community setting.

As hard as it is to accept sometimes, most people in your immediate life will never understand the experience of being trans because they aren't. So while you can hope that they accept you the way you are regardless of their understanding, letting go of the need for everyone to understand you to feel happy in your experience is extremely important.

Not everyone will understand you, and that's okay. There is a whole world of LGBTQ+ people showing up for each other, supporting each other, and ready to embrace you with open arms. Don't under-estimate the powerful role community can play in your journey. It can come in many forms, so these are some of the ways that I recommend:

- **LGBTQ+ community centers:** These buildings within a town or city are dedicated to providing a safe space for LGBTQ+ folks to join in on community-driven activities, workshops, and meet-ups.
- **Social media groups and pages:** Any social media pages that promote acceptance, education, and community engagement for LGBTQ+ folks are a great way to find support.
- **LGBTQ+ organizations:** These are non-profit organizations with various functions related to supporting LGBTQ+ people. Some organizations advocate for

LGBTQ+ rights, while others might have a more specified focus, such as representing and supporting LGBTQ+ parents and families.

Connecting with the LGBTQ+ community and finding the support you need is vital to feeling a sense of belonging along your journey. There are people dedicated to creating the space for us to succeed in a world constantly pushing us down. Don't let yourself be a stranger in a community ready to love and support you. Reach out and know that you will be welcome.

These organizations and groups are here to help you through your transition and other steps you may take down the road. No matter where you are along your journey, there is no better time to connect than now. To help you do that, and to help you see all the support you have at your fingertips, here is a list of the top LGBTQ+ organizations you should know about:

- **The LGBT National Help Center:** This non-profit organization focuses on meeting the general needs of LGBTQ+ people. They have a hotline called the LGBT National Hotline for those seeking immediate support (888-843-4564) and over 15,000 local resources.
- **Human Rights Campaign (HRC):** This is the largest gay, lesbian, bisexual, and transgender advocacy group in America. They have over 600,000 members fighting for equal rights for LGBTQ+ people.
- **Family Equity Council:** This organization focuses on supporting, representing, and connecting LGBTQ+ parents across America. They help build community, educate on LGBTQ+ rights, and support LGBTQ+ families.
- **Transgender Law Center (TLC):** This center is the largest trans-led organization in America. Their main focus is advocating for self-determination in society and the laws

to affirm that. They also help trans people with common legal struggles like changing documentation after transitioning, and more.

- **Pride At Work:** This organization represents LGBTQ+ union members to support equal rights and safe work environments. They help set in motion beneficial union contracts to end discrimination and improve wages for the community.
- **Out And Equal Workplace Advocates:** This organization works exclusively on advocating for LGBTQ+ rights in the workplace. They provide resources and programs to educate companies on equality, and they run events helping LGBTQ+ people succeed in their careers.
- **The Transgender Training Institute (TTI):** This institute is a trans-led national training and consulting service. They provide developmental training for work teams to better educate them on trans communities, as well as training for trans folks to become facilitators of TTI.
- **Athlete Ally:** This organization focuses on making the sports world more inclusive for LGBTQ+ communities. They run education programs at college level, they work to change policies in big sports teams and institutions, and they advocate for LGBTQ+ rights.

These are just a few organizations dedicated to serving the LGBTQ+ community. It doesn't matter who you are, where you're from, or how old you are. There is support out there for whatever you're going through. There are even community organizations for helping elderly LGBTQ+ people with retirement and others for LGBTQ+ people in the military. The level of support for our community is impressive.

Partners

If you are ready to come out for the first time, want to start your transition, or are already out and learning to live more authentically, having a partner in your life that you can trust is a valuable asset. A supportive partner can stand by you on this journey and help you feel loved unconditionally.

However, gender identity and gender roles are essential in any relationship dynamic. You must know that coming out as trans and beginning your transition to match your true identity may shift things in your relationship. It is also possible that it could lead to the end of it.

Once I found the courage to face my partner and tell her that I was trans, I knew that it was not something she would take lightly. Of course, I hoped she could understand, assuming she loved me and not my gender identity, but it was too big a shift away from who she thought I was. So, although we were in a relationship for six years and living together at the time, we decided to end it.

Losing my girlfriend during such a confusing time hurt a lot back then. It still hurts a little now, but I have come to terms with it. The right person would've loved me through the process. But we also can't expect someone we love, who has loved us a certain way for so long, to understand immediately what we're going through and why we must transition.

To some partners, it may feel like they are losing someone they love, although we are simply transforming into our most authentic selves. I urge you not to let the fear of a breakup stop you. *You* are the most important and valuable asset in your life. Don't hide yourself away to hold onto the comfort zone of a relationship.

There is also every hope and chance that your partner will embrace your changes and encourage you to be yourself. A partner worth your time will love you unconditionally. They will stick around if they want to be with you, the real you. Suppose they don't—move on.

Here are some tips to help you come out to your partner in a compassionate way:

- **Prepare:** Before talking to your partner, clarify how you feel and what you want to say. Think about the message you want to convey. Try to be understanding as it might be hard for them to accept such a significant change.
- **Communicate clearly:** Stay calm and sure about what you want to say to communicate as clearly as possible. Open communication is the key to working through problems, significant life events, and stress as a team.
- **Show empathy:** Even though coming out is a big deal for you, it can still shock your partner. You will experience the change as a life-changing event, so try to reassure your partner that it's okay if they feel shocked or afraid of what the change might mean.
- **Give them time:** Reassure your partner that it is okay if, at first, they have trouble accepting and understanding this big shift. Allow your partner to go through their emotions and try to support them by answering any questions they may have. It is common for partners of trans folk to feel misled, so if this is the case, reassure them that you are just changing your presentation to be more authentic. Try to be as transparent about your experience, giving them plenty of opportunity to empathize with you too.
- **Be ready to accept their decision:** No matter how well you present this life-changing information to your partner, there is always a chance that they won't be able to accept it. If that is the case, know that it has nothing to do with you but rather internal conflicts within themselves.

Coming out to a partner can be one of the scariest things you do as a trans person. However, it is always worth it and essential to go through with your transition regardless of what they say. You must be true to yourself before expecting someone else to love you.

If things go well, you can ask your partner to support and love you through the process. And if things don't, try to focus your love on yourself until you are ready to embrace love with someone else again. We all want to feel loved whichever way we are the most comfortable with. Being trans will not stand in your way of love but rather make it more authentic.

If you are single right now and like the sound of having a partner in your life, there are things to consider. Some things you should think about before going ahead with a new relationship include:

- **Know what you want:** Before getting into a new relationship, be clear about what you want from a partner. Visualize the kind of partner you'd like, what values they have, and what traits you strictly don't like. Of course, nobody's perfect, but having some ideas will help you navigate potential partners.
- **Choose when to come out wisely:** It's difficult to accept that some people won't want to pursue a relationship with you once they know you're trans, but it's often better to find out sooner rather than later. Of course, it is up to you to come out when you feel comfortable but keep in mind that it may hurt more to be rejected further into a relationship once you've grown deeper feelings for someone.
- **Get good at talking openly:** Communication is important in any relationship, but being trans comes with additional needs and nuances. Practice talking openly with your partner from the start, and make sure you are with someone comfortable communicating their needs in return.
- **Be straightforward with your boundaries:** Being trans can also come with unique limits and physical needs. For example, if you are a trans man with breast tissue, you

may not feel comfortable holding a tight front-on hug. Identify your boundaries regarding your body and personal space and communicate them with your potential partner.

- **Be patient, but know when it's not working:** Any good relationship takes time to unfold and develop, and that might be especially true if you're trans. For example, maybe you've found someone excellent and need to explain much new information to them regarding your identity. In this case, it could take some time for them to accept and understand you better. However, look out for signs of disrespect, loss of interest, and abuse. Look for signs that the relationship is not working before wasting your time and getting stuck in something unhealthy.

Navigating relationships as a trans person has an added difficulty that may sometimes feel disheartening. But it would be best to take care of your happiness before worrying about being single. Enjoy the ride as long as a partnership is healthy and contributes to your and your partners' growth! But be honest with yourself, and put your well-being first.

Educators

Attending classes in any form will require you to come out to your educators to be respected and feel like you can be yourself. Many teachers or educators are well-versed in gender diversity and under-stand the importance of respecting someone's pronouns and gender identity.

As with anyone else in your life, there is still the possibility that an educator might not respect your diversity. Their disrespect could be because of political or religious beliefs and a lack of education and support from government enforcement. In the US, some states allow educators to practice respect for transgender folks, while other states, like Florida, strictly forbid any inclusion of gender diversity in the school curriculum.

It certainly isn't fair that some transgender people go to schools where gender diversity is left out of the curriculum and denied. However, to help you cope with this ignorance, it's best to be aware of it and prepare yourself. Here are some things you could do if an educator is disrespectful about your gender diversity:

- **Know your rights:** Understanding your rights as a trans person will help you stand firm against someone trying to disrespect you. You're less likely to face unfair treatment if you are confident and know how others should treat you.
- **Assert your needs:** If an educator continues to use the wrong pronouns after you've come out to them, remind them of your correct pronouns each time. They may be forgetful, but if they're refusing to use your pronouns, correcting them might persuade them to change their mind.
- **Get help:** Sometimes, the lack of inclusivity from an educator is nothing more than ignorance, but sometimes it can be destructive to trans students. If you feel blatantly disrespected by an educator because of your gender identity and have grown uncomfortable in their class since coming out, don't be afraid to speak out about the treatment and get help from other faculty or authorities.

You have every right to an education as anybody else. Don't make yourself small or feel like you have to hide your identity just because you are a student. You deserve to be respected and acknowledged for who you are in every aspect of your life. Understand that you might not be treated fairly because of your gender diversity, but know it isn't right, and you can stand up for yourself or get help until you are respected.

. . .

Work

It's sad that trans people face severe repercussions at work after coming out publicly. Unfortunately, much like when dealing with educators and other professionals who refuse to respect transgender people, many trans people face serious push-back at their place of employment. Here are some everyday things that may happen:

- Employers and co-workers might not respect correct pronoun use.
- Employers may "out" trans employees to their co-workers without allowing the person to come out when they are ready.
- Employers or colleagues may refuse to use a new name unless the legal procedure for the name change is completed.
- Trans employees may lose their jobs or struggle to find work because of their gender diversity.

Please take this information in your stride. Don't let it overwhelm or cripple you in fear or hold you back from living your authentic life. You are not the problem for coming out and wanting to live authentically. If other people want to disrespect you, be stubborn in their beliefs, and do things that negatively impact your career, relationships, or self-esteem, it has nothing to do with you. Instead, it has everything to do with their biased opinions on what is "right."

Once you're caught in this unemployment cycle, getting yourself back on your feet can seem almost impossible. But I don't want you to lose hope. Instead, I want you to know that it may take some time, but there is a way out. The most important thing you can do is stay true to your journey, despite any difficulty you may face.

Don't put your transition on pause out of intimidation from a boss. Don't hide behind your desk and put up with disrespect. And never, for one second, doubt that coming out was a mistake. Again, the problem is not with you; it's with the people refusing to have a sense of humanity in the workforce.

If you are left feeling helpless or stuck in a job, you can reach out to the various LGBTQ+ organizations dedicated to standing up for your rights as a trans person. Call the LGBT National Hotline, get in touch with Pride At Work, or even contact one of the various law institutions like the Transgender Law Center (TLC) for assistance if you were wrongfully dismissed. You have more power than an employer wants you to believe.

Self

Out of all the relationships you will encounter, your relationship with yourself is the most important. No matter what you do, you can't force others to understand and accept you. Likewise, you can't force others to be supportive if they're stuck in a binary mindset that doesn't have room for your divergence.

How much you educate, stand up, or fight for acceptance doesn't matter. There will always be people in your life, maybe even family and friends, who refuse to understand or embrace gender diversity. That is why you must be the support system you need. Perhaps at this point in your journey, you have no one. I'm here to tell you that's okay. You will be okay, even if you're the only one rooting for your transition right now. You'll be okay if you focus on giving yourself the love and care you so desperately need.

It took me many years to realize, but if I hadn't started loving myself when I did, who knows where I'd be right now? I might have never begun my transition if I had waited for the approval of all my loved ones and others around me.

When you build a solid foundation of love and acceptance for yourself, flaws and all, your validation will be enough. You can let go of what others think, whether others support you or if you're loved. The one person who matters the most in this world loves you, and that's enough. Your love is the love that will heal your wounds and make you feel worth something. No one else can do that for you but yourself.

So, before we end this chapter, I want to make sure you're equipped to love yourself the way you deserve. So, take note, and start with these simple forms of care:

- **Take care of your body:** Fuel your body with healthy foods, ensure you're eating enough, drink water, and move your body every day in whatever way you can. Your body is your foundation for a healthy, happy life.
- **Take care of your mind:** Check your mental health and ensure nothing's out of hand. If you suffer from anxiety, depression, or other mental illness, keep track of how you're coping. If needed, reach out for professional help, or contact someone in your support system. If you need some downtime, take it. You can't be happy if your thoughts aren't healthy.
- **Surround yourself with positivity:** Make sure you're mostly consuming positive media. Stick to movies that make you feel good, inclusive podcasts, and uplifting music for a while.
- **Live your truth:** Express yourself authentically without worrying about what others think. If you're living your truth, feeling confident in your skin, and embracing your diversity, it won't matter what anyone thinks because you're happy being you.

While you focus your energy on healing, embracing your trans identity, and becoming your most authentic self, you may face adversity in almost every area of your life. Try to focus on your well-being for now and mend the relationships that matter when you're ready. Your relationship with yourself is your priority.

A significant area of struggle to understand along your journey, especially after coming out and starting your transition, is gender dysphoria—something you shouldn't face alone. That's why this next chapter is all about gender dysphoria, how to know if you're suffering from it, and the dangers of leaving this common trans-related struggle untreated.

6

UNCOVERING GENDER DYSPHORIA

I want to reiterate two things from the previous chapter worth repeating: "Your body is your foundation for a healthy, happy life" and "You can't be happy if your thoughts aren't healthy."

Gender Dysphoria can feel different for everyone, but it's rooted funnily. Gender Dysphoria isn't only a feeling in the mind or a feeling in the body. It's a strange sensation caused by a disconnect between the two. That means you can't eliminate it by simply caring for your mind, body, or even both. You must treat it as something else entirely, like a stone painfully wedged between your inner identity and outer appearance.

Before starting my transition, I coped with gender dysphoria by taking drugs and living recklessly. I drowned the feelings out in every way I could. I did everything besides stop and listen to the voice in my head telling me I was different. I was scared to admit the truth to myself, let alone others. I could feel the rock of dysphoria digging into my identity, trying so desperately to surface what I was hiding. So I continued to ignore it. Maybe I was smiling on the outside, but the anxiety of not living my truth, not expressing the gender I knew I was on the inside, was killing me.

Since transitioning, my mind, body, and soul feel connected to my identity. I feel whole, authentic, and at peace in my body. Of course, I still have days where that isn't the case, but for the most part, transitioning has put me on the path of self-acceptance. I never thought I could be this happy. But this chapter isn't about me. This book isn't about me. It's about you.

Let's uncover the truth and start understanding how to overcome it. As impossible as it may seem, I'm living proof that you can move past your gender dysphoria and finally live the happy, whole life you deserve. But before we can do that, how do you know that it's gender dysphoria you're experiencing?

Gender Dysphoria: A Definition

Knowing what gender dysphoria is is the first step to uncovering it. When experiencing gender dysphoria, there is a disconnect between gender identity and one's assumed gender. It refers to the distress or discomfort associated with that incongruence.

Although gender dysphoria is diagnosable by (DSM-5) the Diagnostic and Statistical Manual of Mental Disorders, it is not an actual mental disorder.

However, being trans and not feeling like you can embrace your true identity can have serious consequences. I'm talking about that uncomfortable rock between your gender identity in the mind, and the gender characteristics and expression of your body.

It can manifest itself in many ways, differing from person to person. It also doesn't have to be happening consistently for days on end for it to be a problem. The experience is different for everyone so don't discount your experience just because it may be mild or inconsistent.

Imagine a puzzle with different pieces that fit together to create a complete picture. Each puzzle piece represents a person's biological sex assigned at birth, which is typically either male or female. However, some individuals may experience a deep sense of discomfort or disconnect between their assigned sex and their internal sense of gender identity. This mismatched feeling is analogous to trying to fit a puzzle piece into the wrong spot, where it doesn't align or complete the overall picture. Gender dysphoria is a term used to describe this distress or unease caused by the misalignment between one's assigned or assumed sex and their gender identity.

To me, gender dysphoria feels like I've got a sticker on my forehead that reads "Imposter." I know I'm valid in my trans experience, but dysphoria can make you feel wrong, mismatched, and out of place. I feel like the spotlight's on me and everyone around me is noticing that I'm trans, but not in a good way, in a way that paints me as the spectacle. It makes me feel like my transition isn't enough and like my body still doesn't belong to me.

To uncover gender dysphoria for yourself, identifying what it feels like for you is key. So, let's go through some of the most common symptoms and experiences that often come with it:

- Having a strong desire to be the opposite gender.
- A sense of being trapped in the wrong body.
- Intense discomfort when looking at or cleaning one's genitals.
- An intense fear or repulsion against developing secondary sex characteristics after puberty.
- Knowing that your inner thoughts and feelings are like those of a different gender.
- A deep desire to have the body, sex organs, or secondary sex characteristics of a gender other than their assigned birth sex.
- Having a strong desire to be treated as a different gender than the one you were assigned at birth.

Gender dysphoria can happen only for a few moments at a time or last the entire day or more.

After transitioning to the point that I have, I don't experience as much dysphoria. When I do experience dysphoria, it is mainly due to my chest. I suddenly feel like my chest doesn't match the standard of what a masculine chest should look like. But I am much better equipped to handle these feelings than when I first transitioned. I want you to feel confident about handling gender dysphoria too. Even though the pain of dysphoria might hit the same each time, knowing how to move past it will be your superpower.

Addressing Triggers For Gender Dysphoria

Before you can move past dysphoria and learn how to cope healthily, you must understand what is causing it. I will refer to the things that cause moments of gender dysphoria as triggers. Triggers are the moment, memory, stimulus, or feeling that suddenly causes dysphoria to arrive. There is no limit to what this can be.

But trans people don't necessarily feel dysphoria all the time. The experience is generally triggered by something that brings their attention to the disconnect within them. For example, the dysphoria is probably not there when you're at home alone, enjoying some alone time in your comfiest clothing, doing something you love. But when you, for instance, look in the mirror and see boobs where you feel you should see a masculine chest, dysphoria arises. In this case, looking in the mirror was the trigger.

Some examples of potential triggers for trans people include:

- **Looking in the mirror:** Seeing your body and feeling disconnected from how it looks. For example, if your body looks more feminine or masculine than how you perceive yourself inside.

- **Getting dressed:** Undressing and seeing unwanted gendered features on your body, or dressing up to go out with friends and not resonating with your appearance. For example, maybe you want to wear makeup and something more feminine, but your friends perceive you as a man, so you start to feel dysphoric.

- **Being misgendered:** When someone perceives and addresses you as the opposite gender to your gender identity. It is one of the most painful triggers that create great inner turmoil for many trans folks. For example, if your friends continue to talk about you as "he," even though you've come out as a trans woman.

- **Seeing other trans folks:** Sometimes, being around trans people can trigger gender dysphoria. For example, if you are transitioning from male to female and see other trans women further along, you may feel envious of their progress and unhappy about your own.

- **Hearing your voice:** If your voice sounds too much like the opposite gender, it could trigger dysphoria to hear your voice. I experienced dysphoria over my voice my entire life; I just didn't know what the feeling meant or why I was feeling it.

- **Physical intimacy:** Any physical intimacy between you and another person may trigger dysphoria. Even a hug could bring awareness to your body and remind you of gendered traits you aren't comfortable with. Further intimacy, like sex, could trigger so much dysphoria that you may avoid it altogether until you feel more comfortable in your skin or find the right partner.

- **Hearing your dead name:** After coming out and potentially changing your name, hearing your dead name can trigger painful dysphoric memories from before. For example, if you bump into an old school friend and they introduce you to someone by the name they remember you by, it could be a severe trigger for an episode of dysphoria.

- **Intimate conversations:** Some trans people experience gender dysphoria during specific personal discussions. For example, if you feel disconnected from your sex characteristics and sex organs, a conversation about sex, bodies, or genitals can trigger dysphoric thoughts and feelings.

- **Specific clothing:** Clothing is often gendered, which can trigger gender dysphoria. For example, you wear clothing that doesn't match your gender identity. Clothes can also become a trigger if it brings your attention to your body, such as wearing tight clothing.

- **Introspective thoughts:** If you have not come out to yourself or others yet about being trans, having introspective thoughts about yourself and your identity can trigger you. Being faced with the truth about who you are is also why many trans people turn to escapism like drugs or alcohol to resist introspective thinking.

- **Something unexpected:** It's possible to experience gender dysphoria for an unknown reason. It could feel as though it hit you out of the blue. However, there is likely still a trigger for the feeling. Still, it isn't obvious such as a thought, memory, smell, or sensation that reminded you of your inner identity or a traumatic memory from before your transition.

There are so many things that can trigger gender dysphoria. Some things, such as trauma, can contribute to the severity of the experience but are not usually the sole cause of the problem. Gender dysphoria is complex and multifaceted.

I don't expect that you'll understand your triggers right away. You might relate to some of the triggers listed above or connect to none of them. Either way, your gender dysphoria is worth paying attention to. It also doesn't matter how mild or severe your experience is; any gender dysphoria is worth improving and resolving.

However, the trick to overcoming this uncomfortable experience is not to avoid any triggers. Instead, first, the most important thing you can do is resolve your triggers' root cause—your discontent with your assigned gender.

What I mean by that is not to become comfortable with your assigned gender but to start embodying the gender you know you are. Once you've identified your triggers, you should work to resolve them as much as possible and start doing things that encourage gender **euphoria**.

Gender euphoria will be a beacon that guides you to living more authentically. It is the opposite of gender dysphoria and is the feeling of intense joy after having a gender-affirming experience, for example, when a trans man gets a compliment about his high fade haircut or when a trans woman goes out in heels for the first time. Any gender-affirming experience that gives you a sense of euphoria triggers this positive feeling.

By paying attention to the things that give you the satisfying feeling of being in line with your gender identity, you can learn what identity shifts you genuinely want and need. Focus on the things that bring you the most joy and gender affirmation, and you will start to combat gender dysphoria.

Of course, I'm about to get much more technical about what you can do to treat gender dysphoria, but knowing yourself and knowing what experiences feel healthy and uplifting for you is a significant compass to guide you along the way.

Before we get into the many treatment options and decisions you can make to improve the severity and recurrence of gender dysphoria, it's important to understand something: Your treatment journey will be unique. Every person struggling with gender dysphoria will have individual triggers to uncover and will respond best to a unique set of treatment options. So, keep that in mind as you finish the chapter and note which options are most comfortable for you.

There are two main types of treatment for treating gender dysphoria—medical and non-medical transitioning. Most trans people choose a combination of options from both types to feel they've successfully transitioned to their true gender. But there is no right or wrong way to transition. You can choose to have a fully non-medical transition or include as many medical treatments as you need.

Non-Medical Transition Treatments

At the start of your transition, you might want to go through some non-medical treatment options before considering medical options. Many trans people choose non-medical options only, and others start their transition with a combination of both medical and non-medical options. The decision is entirely up to the individual.

For some people, a medical transition is impossible, and non-medical options are their only option. Either way, any change is valid. Non-medical options are plentiful and can provide significant relief from gender dysphoria if not complete relief for some. Here are some of the options you have:

- **Psychotherapy or counseling:** Therapy is a valuable component of any transition. A good therapist or team of therapists can help support you along your transition journey. Talking to a therapist can help you overcome complicated feelings, negative experiences, past traumas, and anything that will help you overcome your challenges and step into your authentic self with more clarity and mental strength.

- **Cosmetic changes:** These include any non-medical changes you can make to your outer appearance, such as growing or cutting your hair, wearing clothes that better reflect you, wearing or refraining from makeup, and more.
- **Exercise:** You can use exercise to help change your physical frame to reflect your identity better. For example, lifting weights to build muscle or losing weight to slim out your frame. Exercise can sculpt your body to give you a more masculine or feminine frame depending on how you use it.
- **Natural body changes:** Use your body's natural features to match your gender identity. For example, growing or cutting various body hair.
- **Social and legal changes:** You can make a few social and legal changes, including changing your pronouns publicly, changing your name, and changing your legal documents to reflect your gender identity instead of your assigned gender.
- **Voice training:** Many trans people are unhappy with the pitch of their voice, especially trans women whose voices are not raised by hormone therapy. Hormone therapy can deepen the pitch of a trans man's voice but not a trans woman's. If you are unhappy with your voice, you can attend vocal training sessions to help train your voice to sound more fitting to your identity.
- **Practical training:** This type of training is designed to help you adjust to the social changes you may go through when transitioning to another gender socially. The social dynamics can be very different between men and women, and this training can help you best navigate the change.

Non-medical options form a significant part of a healthy transition. Don't overlook giving them a try before moving on to medical treatments. Even if you are sure about wanting to transition medically, non-medical options lay an excellent foundation for medical possibilities to build upon.

Medical Transition Treatments

Before I discuss the many medical options available during your transition, I want you to feel confident that whatever you decide to do, you should stand firm in your choices. There is no rush, even if you take your time to choose or only want a specific surgery at a certain age, as long as you are considering your needs and backing them up by transitioning how you truly want to. Don't let fear or negative comments stand in your way. Your comfort with the procedures and your needs come first.

Just think about Sonny and Cher's son Chaz Bono. He went through life in the public eye as a young girl, the daughter of two famous musicians. Then, in his 30s, he came out as a lesbian and stood tall in his identity despite his mother's shock. Even though he was in a relationship with a woman he loved, he decided to finally come out as trans and begin his transition, willing to risk losing her to be true to himself.

He began hormone therapy and later had top surgery to masculinize his chest area. He has since been thriving and open to the public about his improved sex life with his partner, who stayed with him during his transition. He has also spoken openly about the improvement she's seen in him since he transitioned.

So, don't let the information in this section intimidate or overwhelm you. First, gain an understanding of what's possible, then see where your needs and comfort zone meet amongst these options.

- **Hormone replacement therapy (HRT):** Also known as gender-affirming hormone therapy, HRT is a treatment that doses the body with gender-specific hormones to help the body develop more physical features of the person's gender identity. For example, those transitioning from male-to-female will take feminizing hormones such as estrogen and testosterone blockers, and those that are female-to-male will be prescribed the masculinizing hormone testosterone.

HRT is a highly effective way for trans people to develop more physical characteristics associated with their true gender. It can help trans men grow facial hair, shift muscle mass, and deepen their voices. It can help trans women develop body curves and breasts, have softer skin, and decrease masculine body traits like erections, body hair growth, and the size of testes.

- **Gender affirmation surgery:** There is a long list of gender-affirming surgeries you can consider to get your desired physical appearance. These include surgeries for trans men, trans women, and non-binary folks. In addition, surgical transitioning can consist of various surgeries for one person or only a single procedure.

Everyone doing a medical transition's needs will be different. For example, some folks might undergo multiple surgeries until they feel complete, while others might be happy with HRT alone.

Either way, learning about what surgeries are available to trans folks and what some folks might need to feel like their transition is complete is valuable to you. Knowing what your options are and understanding them will help you make more informed choices along the way. Here are the surgery options most associated with trans men and the options most related to trans women.

Surgery for trans men:

- **Bilateral Mastectomy:** Breast removal and chest reconstruction (nipple repositioning or dermal implants and tattoo).
- **Gender Reassignment Surgery:** There are multiple procedures included in this term, such as a hysterectomy (removal of womb and ovaries), phalloplasty or metoidioplasty (surgical construction of a penis), scrotoplasty (construction of a scrotum with testicular implants), and a penile implant (giving function to the penis).

Surgery for trans women:

- **Facial Feminization Surgery (FFS):** This can include moving the hairline, facial filler, and jaw and chin reshaping.
- **Breast Augmentation:** Adding breast implants to the chest. It's not about having large breasts but about creating a feminine figure.
- **Gender Reassignment Surgery:** Multiple procedures are included in this term, such as a penectomy (penis removal), orchidectomy (removal of testes), vaginoplasty (vaginal canal construction), valvuloplasty (vulva construction), clitoroplasty (clitoris construction).

Bear in mind that some non-binary folks may need to undergo certain medical or surgical procedures to feel comfortable in their bodies, too, such as a mastectomy or hormone therapy. You should also be aware that there are risk factors to medical transitions, including side effects from HRT and the potential for complications with surgery.

Listening to your surgeon or doctor about the risks is best. Any good practitioner will be honest with you. However, there are also risks to avoiding a transition and ignoring your gender dysphoria as a trans person.

The Risks Of Ignoring Gender Dysphoria

Seeing all the steps you can take to physically appear and see yourself as the gender you feel on the inside seems overwhelming. I get it, there are scary risks involved in most surgeries, and hormone therapy is not something to take lightly.

On the other hand, coming out as trans and sticking to a non-medical transition also comes with risks and challenges. Maybe you'll face bullying or lose lifelong friends. There's no easy way to look at it; our society has much to learn and a long way toward inclusivity.

But what if you do nothing? Why not suck it up and stay exactly the way you are? Safely hiding behind a healthy body and an identity that everyone around you naturally accepts. So what's the problem?

Well, I'm going to be honest with you. As difficult as the journey ahead may seem, doing nothing is even more challenging. Like picking a rosebud before it blooms, taking no action and staying hidden away will only stop you from flourishing. It seems like a considerable risk to transition, but the real threat is living your life unauthentically. You have to focus on being authentic to be happy. Authenticity breeds truth, and you can't have true happiness without that.

If you decide to stay put, ignore the screams within you, and go through life pushing down your gender dysphoria to save yourself the trouble of facing your fears, there are some potentially life-threatening consequences. Some risks of ignoring gender dysphoria include:

- **Worsening symptoms:** Ignoring gender dysphoria can exacerbate the severity of the feeling, leading to worsened symptoms of psychological distress.
- **Psychological distress:** Untreated dysphoria can cause severe and uncomfortable psychological symptoms such as depression, anxiety, shame, isolation, etc.
- **Decreased functioning:** Coping with prolonged psychological distress can interfere with focus, energy levels, and daily functioning. It could get in the way of school, work, household tasks, self-care, and relationships.
- **Self-harm or injury:** People may feel a need to escape or numb their dysphoria with self-harming behaviors like drug abuse, recklessness, over or under-eating, and self-injury.
- **Suicidal thoughts and feelings:** Without treatment, gender dysphoria can trigger thoughts of suicide as people hope to relieve their suffering. These thoughts can be life-threatening if left untreated.

This chapter discusses an overabundance of treatment options and steps to relieve gender dysphoria about one's body and appearance. However, there is one thing missing.

We've spent this chapter rebuilding your foundation as a trans person so that you can feel grounded and happy in your true identity. But what about your mind?

If your body is your foundation for a happy life, and you can't be happy if your thoughts aren't healthy, how do these treatment options serve your mind? The truth is, they don't take you all the way. Sure, you can transition as much as you'd like physically, but if your mind isn't serving you, you'll never be happy with any of it.

Transitioning often takes longer than we wish and involves a lot of complex changes and interactions with others. That's why once you've started treatment to help your outside match your inside, you must master gender dysphoria with your mindset above all else.

The strength and resilience of your inner identity will take you to your happiest, most authentic self. So, turn the page, and be prepared to see your transformation through with a guide to coping and thriving as a trans person.

7

MASTERING GENDER DYSPHORIA:
A GUIDE TO COPING AND THRIVING

Watching the foam pattern swirl as I stirred my morning coffee, my thoughts turned negative. It was a couple of months after I came out to my now ex-girlfriend, and I was living in an apartment alone. The silence was deafening.

"Why am I so pathetic."

"Maybe I should've just kept my mouth shut."

"I'm better off alone."

"I deserve this.

The thoughts continued to spiral in my head. Even though I was supposed to be "out and proud," depression still had a tight grip on me. Sprinkle a daily dose of anxiety, undiagnosed ADHD, and isolation in the mix; it is a recipe for disaster. The only thing keeping me moving forward was my doctor's appointment that afternoon. I was officially about to start female-to-male hormone replacement therapy (HRT), and I couldn't wait. I thought it would be the ultimate cure for my gender dysphoria.

Three months later, I started to notice a few minor changes in my body. I didn't have too much facial hair yet, but I could hear my voice starting to deepen, and my experience as a woman was coming to a welcomed end. However, although I felt good about my progress and was well aware that my HRT results would take some time, I was still unhappy.

Starting my medical transition had little effect on my mental health. There was much more going on in my life than my body not reflecting my gender identity. As a result, my dysphoria was still out of control.

Being trans is more than changing your body and clothing. If your mind isn't right before your transition, there's a good chance transitioning isn't going to solve that—at least not on its own.

At the time, I hardly had any support for my transition. Instead, some of my family and friends were a constant trigger for dysphoria. They couldn't get behind my identity, they misgendered me all the time, and they even made me question the validity of my experience. Doubting my own identity was worse than anything.

Looking back and comparing myself then to who I am now, I feel immensely proud of my journey. I can safely say that my depression and anxiety are minimal, I'm managing my now-diagnosed ADHD, and it's been some time since gender dysphoria was a real problem. Yet, the contrast still takes me by surprise.

But how did I get here? What did I do to come this far and admit happiness to you so effortlessly? Remember the quote from Chapter 5, "You can't be happy if your thoughts aren't healthy." Here is where that comes in.

Being aware that the power of your mind can influence the success of your journey is critical. With a strong sense, it will be easier to let the pressure of conforming get the better of you.

I will show you how to make your mind a fortress. Your inner stability must shine through no matter where you are on your trans journey. Whether you're just becoming aware of your diversity or a couple of years into your transition, your mind will set the tone for your experience.

It took me a lot of self-reflection and growth to start respecting my true identity. I denied and resisted it for as long as possible but had to choose: did I want to keep hiding away and talking down to myself until death became the sweeter option, or was I prepared to fight for my place in this world? **I chose to fight.**

After a solid couple of years from that day in the kitchen, stirring my coffee and repeating the most defeating thoughts to myself, things are very different now. Today, I fully respect and own my identity as a transgender person. I love who I've become, and I'm proud of the work I've put in to get here. I'm happy where I am and excited about where I'm headed. Of course, my journey is still in progress, but that's part of the fun.

Working on my mindset and making essential changes to my environment have brought me to a place where I'm finally comfortable just being me. I've had to discover my boundaries, cut off people no longer serving my journey, and fight to become the best version of myself. But, through the loss and struggle, it was worth it.

Among so many other factors, my willpower ultimately pulled me through. But I like to think of well-being as a cycle. Everything you do to counteract negative influences on your life snowballs into the next until you notice a lasting change. The same goes in reverse. If you let negative thoughts, people, and habits into your life, it won't be long until you start to feel low again. That's why this chapter is all about mindset.

How To Master A Growth Mindset

Adopting a growth mindset will help you get your mind in the best condition it has ever been. Initially coined by Standford University Psychologist Carol S. Dweck, the concept of a growth mindset explains that your beliefs about your intelligence, abilities, and talents determine your success. It's when you believe that action can change an outcome.

The opposite of this is a fixed mindset, where you believe that your strengths and weaknesses are permanent and there's nothing you can do to improve. Before I got my mind right, I had a fixed mindset. I always limited myself by seeing myself as inferior and incapable of improving. For example, I saw my gender diversity as a bad thing— something that isolated me from people rather than something that brought the right people to me.

With time and a lot of self-reflection, I developed a growth mindset. I could see how my effort toward my happiness was paying off. Finally, I proved my fixed mindset wrong. My gender dysphoria wasn't an all the time permanent part of my experience; it was possible to over-come it after all.

So, instead of struggling and wondering where to begin, take a moment to review your mindset and start making changes. Ask your-self, "Do I believe I'm stuck the way I am, feeling unhappy, misplaced, and wrong? Or do I believe that progress is possible if I put my mind to it?"

A growth mindset only sees opportunities, no matter where you are in life. If you want to become more confident in yourself and master a growth mindset, here are nine things you can do:

Let positivity fuel you

It's important to view every element of your life as fuel for happiness, like the healthy cycle from which positivity snowballs into positive outcomes. Positivity is like jet fuel toward a happy life, and negativity is like vegetable oil. So choose what you put in your tank wisely.

What I mean by "consume" is anything you put into your body or mind. The food you eat is an obvious example, but why stop there? Take a look at what media, activities, and conversations you consume. Every influence in your life will affect your long-term health and happiness. So, here are some positive switches you can make:

- Educational podcasts make any mundane activity productive.
- Motivational videos instead of celebrity gossip.
- Engaging in intellectual conversations instead of idle chit-chat.
- Eating balanced, nutritious foods instead of take-out and sweets.
- Exercise you enjoy instead of lounging all day on the couch.
- Watch a comedy movie instead of a horror or a drama.

There are so many ways you can fuel yourself with positivity. Don't let this list limit you. Instead, think of ways to switch out habits and behaviors that don't serve you for activities that do—your life and what suits you are unique. You're the only one that can shape it to nurture progress instead of stagnation.

For example, although yoga might be very positive, it won't be for everyone. Like many things listed above, your unique needs determine how you implement positivity. Maybe you prefer bodybuilding, dancing, or acrobatics instead of yoga. Perhaps you can't exercise the way other people do. It's up to you to choose what will benefit your life and what you need to leave in the past.

Overcome limiting beliefs

Holding onto limiting beliefs prevents you from developing a growth mindset. It's as simple as that. Maybe you're unaware of the box your views are putting you in, but that's even more dangerous than the beliefs themselves. The first step towards overcoming limiting beliefs is to identify and transform the problem or problems. Limiting beliefs can look like this:

- "I'm too shy to go to the movies alone."
- "My body isn't good enough to swim at the beach/pool in public."
- "No one will like me anyway; what's the point in trying to make friends."
- "I'm too weird to fit in with that group."
- "I'm not smart enough to pursue my dream career."
- "You can't be good at something without natural talent."
- "Only people born into wealth can make something of their lives."

Can you see a pattern here? It looks like this: I'm too X to be able to do Y. Limiting beliefs are usually absolute and leave no room for change or improvement. However, it doesn't always have to be about you, either. You can put limits on other people, your career, and even your environment. For example:

- "My mom is too old-school ever to accept my identity."
- "My house is too small to invite new friends over."
- "Sally's dad always looks at me strangely. He is obviously judging me."
- "No one ever gets a raise being a waitress. My job is a dead end job."
- "Money is evil, and everyone rich did something dirty to get it."
- "The winter cold makes me gain weight every year, no matter what I do."

Can you see how a limiting mindset can sap the joy and growth of almost any situation? Thinking in this way puts a block on possibilities. It leaves no room for life to surprise you and is often a self-fulfilling prophecy. What I mean by that is what you believe is often what comes true.

If you believe something true, your mind will automatically notice things that confirm your beliefs. So if you think your parents will never accept your identity, you will pick up on every ounce of doubt or misunderstanding they show. In the same way, if you hope that your parents will accept your identity one day, even if they are old-fashioned, you will open your heart to the possibility of their understanding and feel happier in your life.

I'm not saying that everything you believe will be true indefinitely. But if you don't leave space for the possibility of something going well for you, how can you expect it to go right? You can't expect others to take your identity and transition seriously if you don't believe in yourself. A limiting mindset will make believing in yourself difficult, but a growth mindset will leave wiggle room for change, hope, and adaptability–three things that are required to improve your life.

Pay attention to your words

Just like we have to pay attention to what we consume, we also have to pay close attention to what we put out. That means paying attention to your words and how they impact your life.

Words have immense power. But that's not just the words you say to others; the words you choose to say to yourself are just as powerful, if not more powerful. It can be something you say aloud or think to yourself. It all matters.

What you say to yourself will govern how you think about yourself on a deeper level. To find out how you feel about yourself, you can look at the way you speak to yourself. For example, have you ever heard yourself say, "I'm such an idiot!" when you make a mistake or use a sarcastic tone with yourself? It isn't exactly pleasant.

If you want to figure out whether or not your tone or words are damaging to your mental health, ask yourself: "Would I say this to a friend?" or "Would I speak to my friend like that?"

If the answer is no, then pay attention to what you say and try to restructure it. Maybe instead of "I'm such an idiot." say something like, "Everyone makes mistakes. I'll fix this." It doesn't help to make the situation worse with negative self-talk.

The way you speak to yourself can also indicate what mindset you have. If your attitude is limiting, you may notice yourself using language like: I can't, I won't, I don't know how. But to nurture a growth mindset, you have to change your language to sound more like I can, I will, I am. Use empowering language when you speak to or about yourself. It may be hard to believe at times, but you are the biggest cheerleader in your life.

Spend time with the right people

Once you've started becoming a better friend to yourself, you'll notice that the way other people treat you becomes more important. When you love yourself, you won't stand for disrespect or bullying.

It's going to be difficult to nurture a growth mindset in yourself if the people you surround yourself with have a limiting way of thinking. People with a limiting mindset often bring us down, squash our bright ideas, and make us feel inferior. That's not going to do you any favors along your journey.

If you want to feel more supported, loved, and valid, the people you surround yourself with will make all the difference. Try to find people that make you light up inside. If you find friends that highlight your life, hold onto them!

Then, even though it might be painful, look at the friends and people in your life holding you back or contributing to your dysphoria. People who trigger your gender dysphoria may not respect your transition or who you are. Letting them go will only benefit you and your transition.

Removing the toxic people in your life respectfully and kindly will make room for the uplifting friends you've been searching for. If you're being bogged down by friends who pressure you to be someone you're not, you won't be able to attract the people who love you for you.

Take the leap of faith, and let go of the people who no longer serve your happiness. I'm not saying you must burn bridges, but you can respectfully distance yourself to honor your needs.

Nurture an abundant mindset

An abundant mindset goes hand-in-hand with a growth mindset. These two mindsets complement each other perfectly. When you pair an abundant mindset with a growth mindset, your growth potential becomes limitless. An abundant mindset believes in unlimited possibilities. If you can nurture both these mindsets simultaneously, you will become unstoppable in your growth and happiness.

However, the opposite of an abundant mindset is a lack mindset. A lack mindset goes hand-in-hand with a limiting mindset. This mindset makes you believe there isn't enough of anything in life. It makes you think that there isn't enough opportunity to go around. A lack and limiting mindset will keep you stuck in the past, unhappy with your life. You won't be able to see the possibilities right in front of you because you won't believe they're there.

The great news about mindset is you can transform it! If it's not serving you, you can work to change it for the better. So, if you have a lack or limiting mindset, open your mind to the possibility of limitless potential. Let an abundant mindset show how much joy you can get out of life.

Learn emotional regulation

Our ability to regulate our emotions is often overlooked when we learn to deal with uncomfortable situations like conflict, rejection, and overwhelm. Instead, we often worry about what to say and rely on fixing our thoughts during these highly emotional moments.

However, it's important for you to consider your emotions before anything else. To overcome emotionally intense situations, it is important to learn how to regulate your emotions. Once you can regulate your emotions, regulating your thoughts and actions becomes much easier.

Think of it like a chain of reactions:

1. Something happens that triggers a response out of you. It generally starts with a powerful emotion that can create a fight-or-flight reaction in our body.
2. You become aware of your thoughts saying negative things, reinforcing your emotional response.
3. If you can't get yourself under control, you might take action and either fight or flee.

Emotional regulation comes into play here. If you can regulate yourself right when you start feeling emotionally overwhelmed, you can nip negative thinking in the bud and stop yourself from doing or saying something you don't mean.

There are many ways to learn emotional regulation, but I recommend practicing mindfulness. You won't be able to regulate your emotions if you don't have a keen self-awareness. Before you can do anything, you must be in touch with your mind and body. A great mindfulness practice that will get you in tune with yourself and your needs is meditation.

Meditation improves decision-making, helps you feel more relaxed, and helps you stay calm in stressful situations. You can start by sitting in a quiet place with your eyes closed and paying attention to your thoughts and emotions individually. If you notice a feeling or thought, don't judge it; observe and allow it to pass.

With meditation, you can learn so much about yourself and your inner world. Use it to become more self-aware and then use that awareness to notice when your emotions are out of control.

Some ways that you can regulate your emotions while in a state of fight or flight include:

- **Grounding exercises:** Take a moment to focus on your five senses.
- **Deep breathing:** Take a deep breath in through your nose, and let it out slowly like you're blowing on soup. Repeat if necessary.
- **Butterfly tapping:** Place your right hand on your left shoulder and cross your left arm to touch your right shoulder. Tap each shoulder with the opposite hand like two butterfly wings, one at a time.
- **Mantras:** Repeat a calming mantra to yourself. Choose something easy to remember in a stressful environment, like, "I am safe," "I am calm," or "I can handle tough situations."

The best way to incorporate emotional regulation techniques is to use a few at once. For example, if you get into a conflict and feel your heart racing and your tears welling up. Take a deep breath and slowly repeat a soothing mantra to yourself as you release the breath. You can include butterfly taps in this routine as well.

Then, once you feel yourself coming out of the fight-or-flight state, handle the situation in a healthier, more authentic way instead of doing so when you're out of control emotionally.

Improve your self-awareness

After starting a meditation or mindfulness practice, your self-awareness will improve drastically. You can further your practice and increase your self-awareness to benefit every aspect of your life by using meditation to become consciously aware of what you want and need out of life.

To avoid letting external input control you, like social media, movies, or family, learn to look within and discover what you genuinely want. Try to find validation and happiness from within before looking outside yourself. Pay attention to the life you're trying to create, and write down what you want.

Ask yourself these questions and answer them honestly and openly:

- What do I want my life to look like in five years?
- Who do I want in my life to be?
- What habits and lifestyle changes do I need to make?
- Why do I deserve to live the life of my dreams?

Use these questions as journal prompts. First, answer them in as many words as you want to and keep the results. Then, when a few months or years have passed, return to this page and journal these questions again. Then, go back to your previous answers and compare them. If you do this, and you've been working to improve your life, I can guarantee the comparison will surprise you. You'll be able to see just how far you've come in the time between.

Visualize your future self

To have a growth mindset, you have to be able to believe a better life is possible. Visualization is a great way to help you see that future as a potential reality. Follow these steps to visualize your future self:

- **Step 1:** Sit in a quiet place where you won't be disturbed for at least 15-20 minutes.
- **Step 2:** Close your eyes and focus on your breathing.
- **Step 3:** As you breathe, allow your thoughts to flow freely. Don't judge them; observe them and allow them to pass.
- **Step 4:** When ready, visualize a doorway. See the color of the door and feel the texture.
- **Step 5:** Open the door and step through it. On the other side of the door is your life in 10 years. You are successful and happy. You're living the life of your dreams.
- **Step 6:** Take in every detail of your future dream life. What does your life look like? How does it feel? Where do you live?
- **Step 7:** Write as many details down about your future dream life when ready. Write down the thoughts you want to have, the feelings you want to feel, and anything else necessary to you.
- **Step 8:** When you're done, spend some time creating a vision board of your future dream life and dream self. Use magazine cutouts, prints, stickers, writing, or whatever you feel represents the life that you want.
- **Step 9:** Put your vision board somewhere you will see it regularly.

Take time to meditate and visualize your future success as often as possible. The more you can *see* your future life, and the more details you can notice about it, the easier it will be for you to believe it's possible. Working on your mindset is essential if you want to see a fundamental shift in your life. Using visualization to help shift your perception and beliefs is an invaluable tool. Plus, it's super fun and can be quite moving!

Embrace imperfection

Finally, you can't have a growth mindset if you're afraid of failure. To build the life you want, you must be willing to embrace your imperfections and the imperfections of life. Nothing in life is perfect, but that's part of the beauty. You can be perfectly imperfect and embrace happiness in its proper form by:

- Accepting your flaws.
- Searching for the silver lining in every situation.
- Letting go of perfectionism.
- Seeing failure as an opportunity for growth.
- Prioritizing consistency over perfection.

These are just some of the ways that you can nurture a growth mindset. From becoming more optimistic about life to embracing your imperfections, you'll soon see that every dark cloud, even the darkest cloud of gender dysphoria, will have a silver lining. Use your mindset to transmute any negative situation into a positive one, or at least use it to help you make it through without succumbing to the struggle.

Your mindset will determine how strong you are in the face of adversity. It is your greatest superpower along this journey. However, no matter how strong you are, there's nothing wrong with a bit of help.

. . .

Additional Assistance

Along with your mindset and the work you put into regulating your-self, there are additional tools you can use to improve your experi-ence of further recovering from gender dysphoria. Some things I recommend trying include the following:

- **Therapy:** Having professional help during tough times can help you make sense of things and get the confirmation you need. Find a form of treatment that works for you. I.e., talk therapy, equine-assisted therapy, trauma release therapy, etc. Therapy doesn't have to be a scary thing; it is there to help you improve your mental health. You can also use a good therapist to help you assess your current health and assist you in your decisions moving forward as you treat your gender dysphoria.
- **Gender-affirming items:** To help your body feel more connected to your gender identity, use gender-affirming items. These include binders, packers, STPs (stand-to-pee devices), breast forms, panty girdles, padded underwear, makeup, clothing, shoes, accessories, hair removal items, hair styling products, and anything else you can use to help you experience gender euphoria.
- **Spend time outdoors:** Nature is a form of therapy in itself. Try to spend time outdoors to help you feel grounded and whole. Nature can take our minds off things in the "human" world, like identity, socializing, family dynamics, etc. You can connect with nature by going for walks, gardening, watching the birds, trees, or stars, caring for an animal, or wading in the ocean or any other natural body of water. The power of nature is limitless. Form a connection there, and you'll never feel alone or like you don't belong.
- **Make room for fun:** Despite the seriousness of gender dysphoria, you have to make room for fun in your life. Make

time for the things that bring you joy, and do something fun every day. Even if you have to schedule it, do it!

- **Get involved:** Humans are social beings, and it isn't easy to heal without the support of others. So, get involved and do something that will surround you with like-minded people. Volunteer at LGBTQ+ organizations or other organizations you're passionate about, and surround yourself with people you can relate to.

You can take action and improve your life in so many ways. You don't have to be stuck with gender dysphoria. By now, I hope you can see how valid your experience is and how you're not alone. You're not helpless. You're not a mistake. You are valid in every way, and so much greatness is on the horizon for you.

Before you go and thrive to the fullest, this next chapter will give you a final breakdown of helpful tips and resources that will take your journey to the next level. The more knowledge you have, the more empowered you will become. So read on!

8

HELPFUL TIPS AND RESOURCES

When I first started my transition, I felt alone in the world. And I don't mean that I was just lonely; it felt like I was having an experience no one else was like I was the only one in the world going through all this. I didn't know how many wonderful, amazing people there were like me.

I went from being isolated, depressed, and confused about what to do to being surrounded by like-minded friends, feeling like myself again, and genuinely being happy. All I could ever want for you is to see the same transformation in your life.

By now, I know you've been through a lot since chapter one, either in your life or internally. But this chapter, the book's final chapter, is here to see you to the end. So please pick this book up and flip to these pages repeatedly in times of need. This chapter is your resource to remind you, guide you, and help you convey the messages you want to convey to others.

So, to help see you on your way, I've compiled a list of tips I know you'll find helpful. You can use these tips to remind yourself of some of the little things worth practicing to support yourself and others in the community, or you can show this chapter to anyone you'd like to help educate. So, as part of the community or as an ally to us, let's get into this chapter's helpful tips and resources.

Best Practice For Handling Pronouns

I know we've been through pronouns in chapter three, but I want to repeat a few tips worth remembering. Whether you are a part of the trans and non-binary community or simply an ally, correct pronoun use is something we have all had to adjust to. I grew up binary and still make mistakes from time to time.

You are not transphobic for making a mistake. Simply correct your errors respectfully and quickly, then move on. If you offend someone, apologize immediately and continue with more caution. But, of course, prevention is better than cure, so here are a few ways to master pronouns:

- **Practice makes perfect:** The more you practice asking someone what their pronouns are, making an effort to use correct pronouns, and finding ways to remind yourself of who uses what pronouns in your life, the easier it becomes to avoid mistakes.
- **When in doubt, use their name:** If you have forgotten someone's pronouns in conversation, don't panic! You can use the person you are speaking to or about's name. In most cases, it works just fine.
- **Pay attention to the crowd:** If you find yourself in a stressful scenario where you've forgotten someone's pronouns AND their name, or you don't know them yet, listen to the people around you. Try to pick up on someone's pronouns by how their friends address them.
- **Use they/them pronouns:** Sometimes, it's not possible to find someone's pronouns before you have to address them

or speak about them. In these cases, use they/them pronouns as a default. Using they/them is an excellent way to fall back on when all else fails, but don't get lazy regarding people whose pronouns you know.

My Suggestions For Finding Gender Euphoria

Along my journey, there have been many instances where I felt detached from my body and dysphoric. But here are some of my favorite tricks to finding euphoria again when you need a pick-me-up:

- **The coffee order trick:** Go to a coffee shop like Starbucks, which takes your order by name. Give them your chosen name when you order, and wait for them to call it out. It will feel good to hear your new name get called out, and they will likely write it on the side of your cup which can be validating.
- **Use technology to your advantage:** Change your name on your computer profile so that when you log in, you'll see your new name instead. Then, give any talking bots you use, like Alexa or Siri, your new name.
- **The name tag tip:** If you go to a social meet-up, event, or LGBTQ+-friendly speed dating function, write your chosen name on your name tag and enjoy hearing people read it out when they greet you.

If you are an ally, friend, or family of someone who is trans or non-binary, here are some things you can do to help show your support and decrease gender dysphoria in your friend or loved one:

- **Say their new name whenever appropriate:** For example, when greeting them, introducing them to others, and asking them a question.
- **Write their chosen name on any wrapped present you give them:** For example, when labeling presents for Christmas or their birthday.
- **Say the correct name when singing happy birthday to them:** For example, if you call your newly transitioning friend on the phone to sing them happy birthday, use their new name to make it count.
- **Be a good listener:** Create a safe and non-judgmental space where your loved one can share their feelings, experiences, and concerns. Actively listen to them without interrupting or invalidating their experiences. Show empathy and validate their emotions.
- **Be mindful of language and behavior:** Be aware of the language and jokes you use. Avoid making assumptions about gender or reinforcing stereotypes. Speak up if you witness others using inappropriate language or engaging in discriminatory behavior. Advocate for their rights and dignity.
- **Support access to resources:** Help your friend or loved one access resources to assist them in their journey. This could include finding support groups, mental health professionals with experience in gender identity issues, or transgender-friendly healthcare providers.
- **Respect boundaries and privacy:** Understand that each person's experience is unique, and not everyone may be comfortable discussing their gender identity openly. Simply respect their boundaries and privacy. For example, don't disclose their trans or non-binary status without permission.
- **Offer practical support:** Provide practical support by accompanying them to appointments, assisting with legal

documentation changes, or helping with clothing and grooming. Your assistance can be precious during their transition process.

- **Stand up against discrimination:** Be an ally and advocate for transgender and non-binary rights. Speak out against discrimination, inequality, and prejudice. Provide support for policies and initiatives that promote inclusion and equal rights.
- **Celebrate milestones and achievements:** Acknowledge and celebrate your loved one's milestones and achievements related to their gender identity, such as coming out, starting hormone therapy, or legal name changes. Your support and encouragement can make a significant positive impact.

Self-Care Through Journaling

Sometimes things are going to get tough. It doesn't matter how well you've been doing or how stable you are; life is full of ups and downs. How you deal with the downs is the most important thing. Self-care is your ticket to healthy coping, and journaling is one of the most effective self-care practices.

Some benefits of journaling include:

- Better overall mental health
- Improved emotional intelligence
- Increased self-confidence
- Higher rate of goal achievement
- A tool for creative inspiration
- Stronger writing skills
- Improved memory
- Better ability to communicate

With so many incredible benefits, why would you not want to try a journaling practice? Of course, journaling is not one-size-fits-all. There are so many great methods to use in a fun, expressive, limitless way. But I recommend trying:

- **The flow of consciousness writing:** This form of journaling allows you to uncover hidden truths from your psyche. Grab your journal and a pen, and write down your thoughts as you have them. Don't think about what you'll write; just let it flow onto the page. Read it back to yourself when you're done, and prepare to be surprised by what you might learn about yourself and how you feel.
- **Journal venting:** You can use your journal to vent as if your journal is a friend that would never judge you. Write down whatever is bugging you, and be as expressive as you want. Burn the pages if you're nervous about people finding what you've written in anger or frustration. The act of burning journal pages is therapeutic in itself. Practice with caution.
- **Clarity seeking:** Your journal can act as a mirror to your inner thoughts. Use your journal as a sounding board to help determine what to do next about a problematic situation. For example, if you're feeling dysphoric, write down how you feel and use your journal to get to the bottom of it to help you find solutions. It's a great practice to relieve stress while being proactive about the problem.

Easy Upliftment With Affirmations

Another self-care practice that you can do on the go is using positive affirmations. Often an approach that goes well with journaling, affirmations are a great way to boost your self-confidence and nurture self-love.

Positive affirmations can be whatever you want them to be, but here are some affirmations I recommend starting with:

- I am worthy
- I deserve authentic, unconditional love
- I love myself
- I deserve safety
- I am at peace with myself
- I have a purpose beyond measure
- My life holds more value than I can imagine
- I am perfectly imperfect
- I am happy
- I can handle any obstacle in front of me
- I am worthy of abundance

The purpose of affirmations is to make them easy to remember so that you can repeat them as often as you like. You can use them in any way that feels the most beneficial to you, such as:

- Saying them out loud in front of the mirror every morning.
- Repeating them to yourself in your mind throughout the day.
- Use them to help you stay regulated during stress, i.e., confrontation.
- Writing them out in your journal every evening.
- Printing them out and sticking them in places around your home where you'll see them often.

Adding positive language like this into your life will help you get used to speaking to yourself and positively seeing yourself. Positive thoughts and words have a massive impact on how you feel and how you see reality. Using affirmations can help you build the amazing life you're capable of living; it all starts from within.

Tips For Keeping Safe

While it's nice to forget about the cruelty of life, your safety counts on being prepared for it. Unfortunately, our sad reality is that not everyone accepts transgender people, and some even strive to hurt us. Because of this, I want to equip you with the top safety tips I can think of:

- **Stay alert:** Don't let yourself be distracted when you're out. Staying alert can look like taking your earphones out, putting your phone away, and being completely present.
- **Do your research:** If you are gender non-conforming, be cautious in areas that are not friendly towards the trans community. Be sure to research new places you visit, and be prepared if you are traveling somewhere with a more conservative culture.
- **Trust your instincts:** When you're out at night, in a new area, or meeting someone new, trust any gut instincts you have. If you don't feel safe somewhere, you likely aren't, and it's better to leave or avoid the situation.
- **Get familiar with the area:** If you are new to a neighborhood, town, or city, take time to get to know the area and learn as much as you can about where to go and where to avoid. If something were to go wrong, it'd boost your confidence if you know the area well enough to get somewhere safe quickly.
- **Project confidence:** How you carry yourself can paint you as an easy target or someone to be left alone. Your body language can do a lot for you in an intimidating area. If you are hunched over, distracted, or looking timid, it can make

you look vulnerable. Be sure to walk and act like you always know where you're going.

- **Use the buddy system:** Always travel in groups, especially in areas not very LGBTQ+ friendly and public restrooms. There is safety in numbers, especially if a group approaches you.
- **Carry a noise-making device:** In an emergency, carry a noise-making device like a whistle or personal alarm. If you encounter someone threatening, you can use a noise-making device to deter them or quickly attract help.
- **Carry a pepper spray or tazer:** This is a less recommended tip. But pepper spray or a tazer can be useful if someone attacks you. The problem with this option is it can give you a false sense of security and sometimes be difficult to use if caught off guard.

These are the basic safety tips you should use whenever you go out or visit a place you don't know well. But there is more that you can do to prepare for the worst.

My goal is not to scare you but to make you aware of your risk level as a trans person. It's better to be aware of and prepare for it than to live in denial. So, to help you get strong and feel confident going out into the world as your authentic self, try these long-term safety strategies:

Take self-defense classes

Whether you learn in person or through YouTube tutorials, self-defense is a significant long-term investment in your safety. You want to know what to do if a predator ever targets you. Most predators are expecting you to refrain from fighting back effectively. I want you to get confident and learn this three-step self-defense protocol:

1. **Be as loud as you can:** Shouting, screaming, or using a noise-maker can help attract the proper attention and get you support. It can also scare off the predator as they won't want any attention drawn to them.
2. **Defend yourself:** Use your head, knees, and elbows wherever possible, as they are your body's hardest parts. You can also try using these self-defense moves: - Bust their nose with the bottom of your open palm. - Poke or scratch them in the eye. - Wristlock them. - Headbutt them with your forehead. - Headbutt them with the back of your head. - Bite them.
3. **Run to safety:** As soon as you're free or get the chance, run away to safety as fast as you can.

Navigate online forums safely

As LGBTQ+ people, it's often easier to meet friends and supportive people online using online forums, Facebook pages, etc. Unfortunately, predators are not only dangerous in person; they can also cause a lot of harm through online platforms. There are also hackers on the internet, trolls, and bullies. To keep yourself safe online, follow these essential tips:

- **Personal information:** Be cautious with how much personal information you give online. Your full name, address, and phone number are enough to do much damage. Your financial information should also be on your red list.
- **Passwords:** Always use a solid and unique password for any account you make online. Refrain from using anything that can easily be traced back to you or guessed, like your birthday, your name, or something silly like "password123."

- **Links and downloads:** Be careful about which links you click on and what files you download from online chat groups. Even the most harmless-looking links or pictures could have malware attached.
- **Privacy:** Proceed cautiously when talking to anyone pressing you for more information than you're comfortable giving. Someone showing too much interest in you and your personal life too quickly is a red flag.
- **Stay public:** As a safety rule, never use private online chatrooms where you have too much one-on-one contact with someone unless that's what you're looking for. Just practice discernment and know that it's easy to get catfished. Private chats leave you at a higher risk of being manipulated and entertaining unwanted contact.
- **Report bad behavior:** Always report suspicious or inappropriate behavior to the forum moderators or the platform's support team. Even if you aren't directly involved, you could save someone else.
- **Protect your identity:** A virtual private network (VPN) can significantly reduce your tracking risk.
- **Trust your instincts:** In the real world and online, your intuition can help tell you when something isn't right. If at any point you feel uncomfortable or off in any way, leave the chatroom immediately.

Again, this information is not to make you fearful of enjoying your life. I want you to be prepared and to feel confident that in the worst-case scenarios, you will know how to handle it. You have just as much right to go out and have a good time as anybody else. Don't let fear stop you; just be aware of the risks and take the necessary precautions.

Helpful Hotlines

Now, before you move on to the conclusion of this book, I want you to promise me something. Promise me that you won't try and go through this alone. Make use of the hotlines I'm about to give you in times of need, and please reach out to your local LGBTQ+ community, even if the closest one you have is online.

The Trevor Project: A non-judgmental hotline for under 25 year olds in need of immediate assistance for any mental health crisis and/or suicidal thoughts. All counsellors on the line have training and are LGBTQ-sensitive.

- Trevor Lifeline: 1-866-488-7386
- TrevorText: Text the word START to 678678
- Both lines are available 24/7

Trans Lifeline: A supportive hotline run by trans people for trans people in the U.S. and Canada. You can call this line for assistance with any crisis such as gender identity struggles or self-harm.

- US Line: 1-877-565-8860
- Canada Line: 1-877-330-6366
- Both lines are available 24/7

Pride Institute: This is a hotline for anyone in the LGBTQ+ community ages 18 and above struggling with chemical dependency or needing mental health referral and information.

- Main Line: 888-616-5031
- Line is available 24/7

. . .

Fenway Health Helpline: This helpline can provide information, support, and referrals to any LGBTQ+ caller. They have various lines you can call.

- LGBT Helpline (25+): 1-617-267-9001
- Toll-free: 1-888-340-4528
- You can call this line from Monday-Saturday from 6 pm - 11pm ET.

- Peer Listening Line (25 and under): 1-627-267-2535
- Toll-free: 1-800-399-PEER
- You can call this line from Monday-Saturday from 5:30 pm - 10 pm ET.

No matter what you're going through, there are people dedicated to helping you. So please don't ever feel like your problems aren't significant enough to call someone or reach out.

I can't tell you how honored I am to be a part of your journey in this way. You're ready to take to your authentic life like a duck to water. So, take a deep breath, turn the page slowly, and let me see you off with all the love and care in my heart, from one trans folk to another.

AFTERWORD

I'm so grateful you are here right now, reading the words on this page. If you're here, you've read through to the end.

Exploring gender identity is a deeply personal and complex journey that I have been privileged to share through this book as a transgender author.

In addition to sharing my own experiences as a transgender person, I have also shared my own experiences about navigating gender identity, including the challenges and triumphs that occur when living authentically as oneself. As a result of sharing these experiences, I hope to provide an understanding and empathy for those who face discrimination, marginalization, and violence due to their gender identity.

This book emphasizes respecting and affirming everyone's gender identity, including using appropriate pronouns and names and creating safe and inclusive spaces. It also means recognizing the diversity of gender identities and celebrating the richness and complexity of the human experience.

You see that there is hope to overcome your struggles with gender identity and dysphoria. You've learned that there are options for you to live your authentic life and be happy. You deserve to be happy. You've learned about your sexuality and how it differs yet relates to gender identity. And you've learned that you are worth every ounce of effort you put into yourself.

Now that you've reached the end of this book, I want you to know that it'll always be here waiting for you again. So whether you're having a bad day, struggling with something we've spoken about before, or you need to feel understood, pick up this book and know that I am here for you amongst these pages.

I hope that you take what you've learned here and apply it to your own life, your own story. I know you must resonate with at least some of mine, so don't be afraid to go out and live yours. Your story is unique and wonderful.

If you want to read more stories like your own and like mine, I've compiled a special book of stories to show you that you're not alone. I want you to know you belong. You can find a copy of *Becoming Me* on Amazon. If it's not out now as you read this, it will be soon.

While you're there, I'd love to hear how this book, "Understanding Gender Identity," has impacted your life. I urge you to leave a review so we can connect. Let's connect so your feedback can help me better support you in the future. I genuinely wish you all the love, wellness, and happiness you deserve. Go out, live your authentic life, and never look back.

PLEASE LEAVE A
REVIEW

Your voice is important and should be heard! By leaving a review, you have the power to inspire, uplift, and guide others who are questioning their gender identity.

★★★★★

REFERENCES

Bringhurst, Robert. *The Elements of Typographic Style*. Version 3.2. Point Roberts: Hartley & Marks, 2004.

The Chicago Manual of Style. 17th ed. The University of Chicago Press Editorial Staff. Chicago: The University of Chicago Press, 2017. https://www.chicagomanualof style.org/.

Vellum Tutorial. Updated regularly. Oakland and Seattle: 180g. https://help.vellum.pub/tutorial/.

Bringhurst, Robert. *The Elements of Typographic Style*. Version 3.2. Point Roberts: Hartley & Marks, 2004.

The Chicago Manual of Style. 17th ed. The University of Chicago Press Editorial Staff. Chicago: The University of Chicago Press, 2017. https://www.chicagomanualof style.org/.

Vellum Tutorial. Updated regularly. Oakland and Seattle: 180g. https://help.vellum.pub/tutorial/.

Geen, J., & Geen, J. (2021). 5,000-year-old 'transgender' skeleton discovered. *PinkNews | Latest Lesbian, Gay, Bi and Trans News | LGBTQ+ News*. https://www.thepinknews.com/2011/04/06/5000-year-old-transgender-skeleton-discovered/

Gender Identity Development in Children. (n.d.). HealthyChildren.org. https://www.healthy-children.org/English/ages-stages/gradeschool/Pages/Gender-Identity-and-Gender-Confusion-In-Children.aspx#:~:text=Gender%20identity%20typical-ly%20develops%20in,sense%20of%20their%20gender%20identity

Haas, A. C., Eliason, M., Mays, V. M., Mathy, R. M., Cochran, S. D., D'Augelli, A. R., Silverman, M. M., Fisher, P. W., Hughes, T. L., Rosario, M., Russell, S. J., Malley, E., Reed, J., Litts, D. A., Haller, E., Sell, R. S., Remafedi, G., Bradford, J., Beautrais, A. L., . . . Clayton, P. J. (2010). Suicide and Suicide Risk in Lesbian, Gay, Bisexual, and Transgender Populations: Review and Recommendations. *Journal of Homosexuality*, *58*(1), 10–51. https://doi.org/10.1080/00918369.2011.534038Kelly, J. (2022, December 7). The Rise Of The Stay-At-Home Dad. *Forbes*. https://www.forbes.com/sites/jackkelly/2022/12/07/the-rise-of-the-stay-at-home-dad/?sh=1d1b4cd37921

Kurth, F., Gaser, C., Sánchez, F. A., & Luders, E. (2022). Brain Sex in Transgender Women Is Shifted towards Gender Identity. *Journal of Clinical Medicine*, *11*(6), 1582. https://doi.org/10.3390/jcm11061582

Prismic. (n.d.). *Myths - Gender Spectrum*. Gender Spectrum. https://www.genderspec trum.org/articles/myths

Purves, D. (2001). *What Is Sex?* Neuroscience - NCBI Bookshelf. https://www.ncbi.nlm.nih.gov/books

Sex differences in brain anatomy. (2020, August 4). National Institutes of Health (NIH).

https://www.nih.gov/news-events/nih-research-matters/sex-differences-brain-anatomy#:~:text=Females%20had%20greater%20volume%20in,processing%20d-ifferent%20types%20of%20information

The Cost of Coming Out: LGBT Youth Homelessness | Lesley University. (n.d.). https://lesley.edu/article/the-cost-of-coming-out-lgbt-youth-homelessness

The Trevor Project. (2021, September 14). *Pronouns Usage Among LGBTQ Youth | The Trevor Project*. https://www.thetrevorproject.org/research-briefs/pronouns-usage-among-lgbtq-youth/

The Williams Institute at UCLA School of Law. (2022, September 27). *How Many Adults and Youth Identify as Transgender in the United States? - Williams Institute*. Williams Institute. https://williamsinstitute.law.ucla.edu/publications/trans-adults-united-states/

Zaliznyak, M., Yuan, N., Bresee, C., Freedman, A. N., & Garcia, M. M. (2021). How Early in Life do Transgender Adults Begin to Experience Gender Dysphoria? Why This Matters for Patients, Providers, and for Our Healthcare System. *Sexual Medicine*, *9*(6), 100448. https://doi.org/10.1016/j.esxm.2021.100448

46,XX testicular difference of sex development: MedlinePlus Genetics. (n.d.-c). https://medlineplus.gov/genetics/condition/46xx-testicular-difference-of-sex-development/#:

Risaschnebly. (n.d.). *Confronting Human Chimerism*. https://askabiologist.asu.edu/embryo-tales/chimeras-human

This glossary of LGBTQ+ terminology is here to provide you with a better understanding of the diverse identities within the community. The glossary includes definitions of terms related to aspects of queer culture. I covered many terms related to gender identity and sexual orientation in chapters 1 and 2.

However, I included the glossary because the book aims to empower readers to communicate effectively and respectfully with people of all gender identities and sexual orientations.

Ally (noun) – A person who actively supports marginalized groups' rights, even if he or she is not a member of the group.

Assigned female at birth/Assigned male at birth (noun) – Infant characteristics, such as anatomical or biological characteristics, are determined by the child's sex. AMAB (assigned male at birth) or AFAB (assigned female at birth).

Bigender (adjective) – A person who has two gender identities combined.

Binding (verb) – Wrapping one's chest tightly to minimize the appearance of breasts. To accomplish this, cloth strips, bandages, or specially designed undergarments, called binders, are used.

Biphobia (noun) – Discrimination, marginalization, or hatred directed at bisexuals or those perceived as bisexuals.

Bottom surgery (noun) – A form of genital surgery in which the results are gender-affirming.

Cisgender (adjective) – A person whose gender identity matches their assigned sex at birth in a traditional sense. In Latin, cisgender means "on the same side as."

Coming out (verb) – The act of identifying and accepting one's own sexual orientation or gender identity (coming out to oneself), and expressing that orientation or identity to others (coming out to family, friends, etc.).

Gender-affirming hormone therapy (noun) – Aligning secondary sex characteristics with gender identity through hormones.

Drag (noun) – Performing as a different gender or multiple genders. Performers can be classified as Drag Kings or Drag Queens.

FTM (noun) – Female-to-male transgender person, who often identifies as a trans man. Individuals who are assigned female at birth but identify as male or on the male-aligned identity. Also referred to as "transmasc" or "transmasculine."

Gender (noun) – Women and men play different roles based on social norms. In the same way sex can be described as feminine, masculine, or androgynous, gender can also be described as feminine, masculine, or androgynous.

Gender affirmation (noun) – Accepting, expressing, and recognizing one's gender identity through social, legal, and/or medical means.

Gender-affirming surgery (GAS) (noun) – Body modifications that align a person's gender identity with their body. The procedures included in GAS are chest and genital surgeries, facial feminization, body sculpting, and hair removal.

Gender-affirming chest surgery (noun) – Removing or constructing a person's chest to align it with their gender identity. Also called a *top surgery*. The following types of chest surgery are available:

- **Feminizing breast surgery:** breast augmentation, chest construction, or breast mammoplasty
- **Masculinizing chest surgery:** mastectomy (removal of breast tissue) and chest contouring

Gender-affirming genital surgeries (noun) – An individual's genitals and/or internal reproductive organs can be aligned with their gender identity through surgery, including:

- Clitoroplasty (creation of a clitoris)
- Hysterectomy (removal of the uterus; may also include removal of the cervix, ovaries, and fallopian tubes)
- Labiaplasty (creation of inner and outer labia)
- Metoidioplasty (creation of a masculine phallus using testosterone-enlarged clitoral tissue)
- Oophorectomy (removal of ovaries)
- Orchiectomy (removal of testicles)
- Penectomy (removal of the penis)
- Phalloplasty (creation of a masculine phallus)
- Scrotoplasty (creation of a scrotum and often paired with testicular implants)
- Urethral lengthening (to allow voiding while standing)
- Vaginectomy (removal of the vagina)
- Vaginoplasty (creation of a neo-vagina)
- Vulvoplasty (creation of a vulva)

Gender binary structure (noun) – There are only two gender categories (girl/woman or boy/man).

Gender-diverse (adjective) – People who do not fit into a binary gender structure (such as non-binary, genderqueer, or gender-fluid people).

Gender dysphoria (noun) – Distress caused by having a gender identity that differs from their sex at birth.

Gender expression (noun) – How a person communicates their gender to others through mannerisms, clothes, speech, and behavior. Cultural, contextual, and historical factors influence gender expression.

Gender fluid (adjective) – A person without a fixed gender identity. An individual with gender fluidity may sometimes feel a mixture of two or more genders. At other times, they may feel strongly aligned with one, at other times with another, and at other times with neither.

Gender identity (noun) – The inner sense of someone as a woman/man/male, girl/woman/woman, or anything else.

Gender role (noun) – Depending on a person's actual or perceived gender, societal norms dictate what behavior is acceptable, appropriate, and desirable. Cultural and contextual factors, as well as interpersonal relationships, can also affect these roles.

Genderqueer or genderqueer (adjective) – A person who identifies as neither male or female within the traditional gender binary. Gender expansive is a term used by some people.

Gender Nonconforming (GNC) – People who do not adhere to societal expectations regarding gender expression or roles.

Heteronormativity (noun) – Describes the pressure society places on people to conform to a stereotypically heterosexual appearance and behavior.

Heterosexual (adjective) – The orientation of women who are primarily physically and emotionally attracted to men and men who are primarily physically and emotionally attracted to women. Also known as straight.

Homophobia (noun) – People who discriminate against, fear, marginalize, and hate lesbians and gays. Individuals, communities, policies, and institutions can be homophobic.

Intersectionality (noun) – The concept that comprehensive identities are shaped by the interconnections between diverse factors such as race, class, ethnicity, sexual orientation, gender identity, physical disability, nationality, religion, and age.

Intersex (adjective) – Characterized by unequal development of reproductive organs, genitals, and other sexual anatomy.

Misgender (verb) – Referring to someone by the wrong pronoun or other gendered terms.

Chosen Name/Name Used (noun) – The name a person goes by and wants others to use in personal communication, even if it is different from the name on legal documents (e.g., birth certificate, driver's license, and passport). Chosen name is recommended over preferred name.

MTF (noun) – Male-to-female transgender person, often identifies as a trans woman. A person born male but who identifies as female or has an identity aligned with that of a female. Also referred to as "transfem" or "transfeminine."

Outing (verb) – Unauthorized or involuntary disclosure of another person's sexual orientation or gender identity.

Non-binary (adjective) – Persons whose gender identity does not fit the traditional gender binary structure of girl/woman and boy/man. The abbreviation NB or enby is sometimes used.

Open relationship (noun) – Relationship between two people who consent to nonmonogamy (i.e., intimacy outside their primary partnership).

Pangender (adjective) – Individuals whose gender identity consists of more than one gender or falls outside of traditional cultural parameters.

Polyamorous (noun) – Having multiple intimate relationships (romantic and/or sexual) consensually. It is sometimes referred to as poly.

Pronouns (noun) – Words you should use when no names are used to refer to a person. Examples of pronouns are she/her/hers, he/him/his, and they/them/theirs.

Queer (adjective) – An umbrella term describing people who think of their sexual orientation or gender identity as outside of societal norms. Although queer was historically used as a slur, it has been reclaimed by many as a term of empowerment. But use caution as some may still get offended by the word.

Questioning (adjective) – A person who is uncertain about their sexual orientation or gender identity.

Sex assigned at birth (noun) – The biological characteristics of an infant determine the infant's sex (male or female). In some cases, sex assigned at birth may also be referred to as birth sex, natal sex, biological sex, or sex; however, it is recommended to use the term sex assigned at birth.

Sexual orientation (noun) – A person's emotional and sexual attraction to others.

Social stigma (noun) – Stereotypes associated with low social status and perceptions of difference between groups or individuals.

Top surgery (noun) – A procedure that affirms the gender of the patient's chest. Refer back to gender-affirming surgery.

Trans man/transgender man (noun) – An individual identifying as male, male, or boy.

Trans woman/transgender woman (noun) – An individual whose gender identity is that of a girl, woman, or female.

Trans feminine (adjective) – Describes an individual assigned male sex at birth who identifies with femininity more than with masculinity.

Trans masculine (adjective) – A person with female sex assigned at birth who identifies more with masculinity than femininity.

Transphobia (noun) – People who discriminate against, fear, marginalize, or hate transgender people. People, communities, policies, and institutions can be transphobic.

Transsexual (adjective) – A term sometimes used in the medical literature or by some transgender people to describe people who have undergone medical gender affirmation treatments (i.e., gender-affirming hormones and surgeries). Use with caution as some find this word offensive.

Tucking (noun) – Generally, this involves hiding one's penis or testes with tape, shorts, or specially designed undergarments.

Two-Spirit (adjective) – An individual who embodies both masculinity and femininity. The term is specifically used by Native Americans, American Indians, and people of the First Nations.

ABOUT THE AUTHOR

Braxton Phoenix Stock is a transgender author breaking barriers and making waves in the literary world. Born and raised in Cleveland, Ohio, Braxton knew from a young age that he was different from the other kids around him. It wasn't until later in life that he discovered and embraced his true identity as a transmasculine person.

Braxton's journey has been one of self-discovery and self-acceptance, and he brings this same honesty and vulnerability to his writing. His book is a testament to the power of self-love and the importance of embracing who we truly are, no matter what society may say.

Braxton's writing is raw, honest, and powerful, offering readers a glimpse into the struggles and triumphs of marginalized and misunderstood people.

While navigating his own journey of self-discovery, Braxton realized the power of storytelling to help others understand and empathize with the experiences of transgender individuals.

Braxton is also a fierce advocate for transgender rights and visibility, and he uses his platform to raise awareness and promote understanding of the issues facing the transgender community. He aims to become a sought-after speaker and educator and is always happy to share his story and insights with others.

Braxton can be found practicing graphic design, watching his favorite TV show Criminal Minds, or spending time traveling when he's not writing. He's also a weight-lifter and fitness enthusiast, using physical activity to stay grounded and centered. As a member of the LGBTQ+ community, he strives to inspire and help others struggling with any aspect of their lives.